Respectful Educators –
Capable Learners

For the children who are special to us . . .

David, Vanessa, Peter, Heather, Adnan, Katharine, Lauren, Georgia, Chevelle, James, Abigail, Alice, Jamal, Francine, Eleanor, Hazel, Sarah, Tamsyn, Liam and Bethany –

with our love and respect

Respectful Educators – Capable Learners

Children's Rights and Early Education

edited by

Cathy Nutbrown

Paul Chapman
Publishing Ltd

Reprinted 2003

Paul Chapman Publishing Ltd
A SAGE Publications Company
6 Bonhill Street
London EC2A 4PU

British Library Cataloguing in Publication Data

Respectful educators, capable learners : children's rights
   and early education
   1. Early childhood education – Law and legislation
   2. Children's rights
   I. Nutbrown, Cathy
   342.4'74

ISBN 1–85396–304–6

Typeset by Palimpsest Book Production Limited,
Polmont, Stirlingshire
Printed and bound in Great Britain

D E F G H   3 2 1

Contents

Acknowledgements   vii
About the Contributors   ix
Starting Points   xiii
 1 The United Nations Convention on the Rights of the Child –
    Progress in the United Kingdom   1
    Gerison Lansdown
 2 Inspection of Early Years in Schools   11
    Jean Ensing
 3 Language, Culture and Difference: Challenging Inequality and
    Promoting Respect   23
    Iram Siraj-Blatchford
 4 Choices in Learning   34
    Wendy Scott
 5 Wide Eyes and Open Minds – Observing, Assessing and
    Respecting Children's Early Achievements   44
    Cathy Nutbrown
 6 Children with Special Educational Needs – a Collaborative
    and Inclusive Style of Working   56
    Elaine Herbert and Jenny Moir
 7 Do We Train Our Early Childhood Educators to Respect
    Children?   69
    Audrey Curtis
 8 Parents and Early Childhood Educators Working Together for
    Children's Rights   81
    Kath Hirst
 9 Their Right to Play   90
    Tricia David
10 Questions for Respectful Educators   99
    Cathy Nutbrown
Endword   109
References   110
Author Index   119
Index   122

Acknowledgements

In any venture that is worthwhile there are people to thank, and I am privileged to be able to thank a good number because I have been supported, helped and encouraged by so many. Saying 'thank you' is important to me, so . . .

Marianne Lagrange from Paul Chapman Publishing has, as ever, provided advice and action when it was needed. The contributors to this book responded to my initial invitation to participate with an enthusiasm that confirmed my conviction that such a book had a place in the literature of early childhood education. They wrote their chapters during the long hot summer of 1995 and though we all write personally there is a common thread of reflection and anticipation in the field of early education and children's rights. I want to thank each one of them for their commitment to this book and their part in a collaborative effort.

The cover design is from original drawings by the children of St Ives Nursery-Infant School, St Ives, Cornwall: my thanks to the children and to the headteacher Irene Tanner for permission to use this work.

I have some special colleagues too, who, in their various ways, have supported my work, listening, commenting, encouraging and knowing when to say nothing! So I say 'thank you' to Margaret Fitter of Sheffield LEA, to Peter Hannon and Elaine Millard at the University of Sheffield and to Dorothy Rouse-Selleck of the Early Childhood Unit at the National Children's Bureau for several conversations that helped to shape my thinking and endorse my convictions.

In writing, reading and thinking about children and childhood I have, this summer, recalled many of the experiences of my own childhood, so now is my chance to thank my mum and dad for the childhood they created for me and the early years of love and learning and family that were my rich beginning. So, to my mum and dad, who answered some questions and let me find my own answers to others.

As well as remembering my own childhood I have been watching my daughter's childhood as it unfolds. She is the best teacher I ever had, her lessons are profound and her insistence on finding out and challenging what she thinks is wrong are a privilege to share. She accepts my offerings and forgives my mistakes, and she made certain that the summer of 1995 included swimming and walking and watching and talking and laughing (as well as writing) so, Bethany Martha, my love and thanks to you. And Andrew, for your consistent encouragement, love and support, I thank you too.

Cathy Nutbrown

About the Contributors

Gerison Lansdown is Director of the Children's Rights Office, which is working to promote the case for a statutory Children's Rights Commissioner. Previously, she worked as Director of the Children's Rights Development Unit, which was created to promote the implementation of the UN Convention on the Rights of the Child in the UK. She is currently on the management committees of the Family Rights Group and Child Poverty Action Group and has also been on the management committees of One Parent Families, Maternity Alliance and Day Care Trust. She has published numerous articles on the subject of children's rights as well as contributing to a number of books on the subject. In 1994 the Children's Rights Development unit produced the *UK Agenda for Children*, a comprehensive analysis of the state of children's rights in the UK.

Jean Ensing is a specialist adviser for the early years. A late entrant to teaching, she taught young children for fifteen years, eight as a headteacher. After her school was inspected she joined HMI. Some five years later, in 1989 she became the HMI with responsibility for under-fives matters. This role included liaison with government departments, voluntary, private and maintained sector providers and the many groups with an interest in the education of young children. After the creation of OFSTED, Jean also trained registered inspectors and from 1993–4 was the HMI observer on the review of the National Curriculum for five- to seven-year-olds.

Iram Siraj-Blatchford is Senior Lecturer in Early Childhood Education at the University of London. She has researched and published widely on early childhood education and teacher education. She has had the privilege of working with young children and parents as a teacher and governor.

Wendy Scott has spent eighteen years as an early years teacher and head of a demonstration school. She has been a senior lecturer in initial teacher training and course tutor for a multidisciplinary advanced diploma, and is now an external examiner for a primary B.Ed. course. She has worked for many years as an early years and primary inspector in London, and is now welcoming the opportunity of gaining experience in many different education authorities through OFSTED inspections. Wendy maintains a range of national links through her membership of the Early Years Curriculum Group and the Advisory Group of the Early Childhood Unit of the National Children's Bureau. As Chair of the British Association for Early Childhood Education, she is active in promoting high quality early education across the country.

Cathy Nutbrown has considerable experience of teaching young children and working with parents, teachers, nursery nurses and other early childhood educators in a range of group care and education settings. Her research interests include children's early learning and development, their literacy and work with parents. Many publications include her first book *Threads of Thinking – Young Children Learning and the Role of Early Education* (PCP, 1994). For four years Cathy has been Vice President of OMEP (UK) (1991–5) an organization committed to promoting optimum conditions for children's living and learning; she has represented OMEP (UK) in several European countries and the USA. She is currently the Development Officer for the Sheffield University–LEA REAL (Raising Early Achievement in Literacy) Project, in Sheffield. *Respectful Educators – Capable Learners* grew out of a conviction that young children are entitled to respectful attention in all they do and that their educators must collaborate to examine their work and beliefs in order to ensure that the rights of the youngest children are secured.

Elaine Herbert has worked in the home setting alongside families and their preschool children with possible special educational needs for more than ten years. At present she is combining her role as Deputy Head of Solihull's Preschool and Home Teaching Service with a part-time secondment to work with the LEA's Parent-Partnership scheme. Her experience has reinforced her belief that in order to maximize the effectiveness of any early intervention programme, it is essential to work closely with parents and other colleagues. She is engaged in research for a higher degree at Warwick University, looking closely at the reactions of fathers to the births of children with special needs.

Jenny Moir began her teaching career as an English teacher in a comprehensive school. A concern for her own young children's development led to an interest and involvement in the playgroup movement. She then joined a team of teachers working with preschool children in special educational needs and finally took up her present appointment in charge of an LEA nursery. Her professional commitment is to enable children to become independent learners and thinkers. Her personal commitment is to work 'to bring about a just and compassionate society which allows everyone to develop their capacities and fosters the desire to serve' (Quaker faith and practice, 1995).

Audrey Curtis was for may years Senior Lecturer at the Institute of Education in London where she was responsible for the early childhood programmes. Since her retirement she has become actively involved with the Council for Awards in Children's Care and Education, working as an external verifier for the national vocational qualification and the new Specialist Teacher Assistant courses. She has also been developing further her interests in the training of early childhood workers overseas. As the European Vice President of the World Organization for Early Childhood Education she travels widely throughout the region lecturing and advising on various aspects of young children's care and education.

Kath Hirst is an early years teacher and researcher. She has been part of the Early Years Advisory Team in Sheffield as an Area Co-ordinator for Under-Fives. She has considerable experience both in teaching young children and in-service training for teachers, nursery nurses and other under-fives educators in a variety of settings. She is committed to working with parents both in school and the community. Her research interests include home–school links, working with parents and early literacy with bilingual families.

Tricia David is Professor of Early Childhood Education at Canterbury Christ Church College. Tricia's publications include *Child Protection and Early Years Teachers* (Open University Press, 1993), and she believes child protection work should be underpinned by a children's rights perspective.

Starting Points

Work began on this book because I believe that the early years of education present a yet to be developed arena for work on children's rights and remarkably few early childhood educators know of, and fewer still are conversant with, the United Nations Convention on the Rights of the Child. Children, from birth, must enjoy their rights and their parents, close adults and educators, working with and for children, must bear some additional responsibility for them and gradually teach them about the responsibilities that accompany rights and help them to learn how to assume and shoulder responsibility. To argue that because young children cannot shoulder responsibility they must not have rights is the position only of someone who continues to seek to deny children the citizenship that is rightfully theirs.

This book is for people who want to address some difficult and penetrating questions such as 'What does a respectful service for children look like?' and 'How do respectful educators behave?' It is a book for people who want to reflect on their own practice and think about their own beliefs.

Views of childhood

The famous and talented sculptor Barbara Hepworth is quoted at the start of this book and I am using her words to affirm the importance of childhood as a time of thinking, formation, foundation and crucial beginnings. Childhood is a time when the path of one's life is influenced and perhaps the course set. It can be a time of active decision-making, engaging relentlessly with minute-to-minute experiences, and making one's mark upon the world, a vital time in the life of every human being.

There is another view of children and childhood which the observations of some individuals, societies and media reports may suggest is still held. Some see children as passive recipients of knowledge, as necessary burdens, as 'adults in waiting, 'adults in the making', 'unfinished'. Hazareesingh et al. (1989, p. 18) considered this when they wrote:

This concept of the child as an 'unfinished' adult shifts the focus away from the child's own intentions, attachments, and strivings – which might in fact open up many learning horizons for the adult, on to an end-product notion of adulthood which is unwisely equated with 'achieved knowledge'. It might be said that this represents a specifically western, 'rationalist' approach to both childhood and learning which by separating the mind from the heart, effectively denies the essential unity of the child.

Perspectives on childhood that include the concept of children as 'adults in waiting' do not value children as learners and therefore create systems of educating, and design curricula, that can be narrow minded rather than open minded and which transmit to children rather than challenge children to use their powers as thinkers and nurture their humanity. Kakar (1981, p. 18) has described the view of childhood in some Indian, Chinese and African cultures 'as a fully meaningful world-in-itself with its own way of being, seeing, and feeling', and it is further argued that 'Indian philosophies, for instance, stress that the child should not simply be "brought up": there is an accompanying responsibility for the adult to enter into the child's mode of experiencing the world.'

Such is the case in some European countries too, in Denmark, for instance, the Children's Welfare Commission has four goals for a policy on children (Villen, 1993):

- to respect the child as an individual in the family and in society;
- to give the child a central position in the life of grown-ups;
- to promote – in a wider sense – the physical conditions in which children grow up;
- to promote equal opportunities, in the conditions of life of children, both in a material and in a cultural sense.

They are still working to achieve those goals but when I visited two kindergartens in Copenhagen as part of an OMEP (Organisation Mondiale pour l'Education Préscholaire) visit I saw children who were valued as children and adults who were respected for the work they did with children. This was evident in beautiful and exciting gardens with ropes hanging from trees, huge sandy areas with planks of wood, crates and tyres for make-believe play on a large scale; garden sheds which were child size so that children could get a bike, a pram or whatever, when *they* wanted it, and be responsible for replacing it after use. Adults were valued to the extent that their staff space (kitchen and rest room) was beautiful too – matching cups and plates, thought-out colour schemes, comfortable and matching chairs, space to relax with colleagues, to discuss and to work. To be a pedagogue (kindergarten worker) was a much sought-after and valued job for men and women. In China the one child per family policy gives us a different perspective on childhood. Such a policy can be seen to deny children the experience of siblings and, it could be argued, overwhelms the single child with adult attention from grandparents, parents and other close family members because this only child is so precious. Durkenheim (1994) has written of the demands made upon children by society and Mayell (1994) explores a range of perspectives on children's lives and considers children's rights in different social contexts.

So society's and individuals' views of children influence the ways in which they are cared for, provided for and educated in their early years. It is important to question the seriousness with which the UK considers children. Does it respect children as people, citizens, able learners, powerful thinkers, feeling human beings? Equally important are the questions to be asked of educators. Do educators watch children's actions and listen to their voices with *wide eyes and open minds*, or are children seen as 'adults-in-waiting' with no real rights, not yet real people, not yet able to think for themselves, no rightful place in the world? Do educators decide *for* children, working with their eyes closed and minds too narrow to accept the view that they are working with powerful and able people, however small and however young they may be?

We must recognize the motivations which drive us to work with and for children and ensure that children's interests are served first and not, as Oldman (1995) argues to be the case, allow this work to become dominated by the interests of adults.

In September 1995 the School Curriculum and Assessment Authority issued for consultation a document describing the desirable outcomes of preschool education (SCAA, 1995). This indicates and is shaped by particular positions on and assumptions of what childhood is and what, at a certain stage in childhood, should be accomplished. The importance of this document was acknowledged both by the chief executive of SCAA, who in the accompanying letter wrote: 'This is an important consultation. There is a lot at stake for all children' and by Sir Ron Dearing, who, in the foreword to the document, said: 'In this consultation we are taking the first step on a matter of much importance to children themselves and for the future of education. The quality of children's early education influences their development and achievement.'

Views of childhood are important when policy decisions affecting a child's childhood and future are being taken and it is interesting (perhaps disturbing) to note that when adults try to make plans for children and the future they sometimes cast blame in the wrong place. An article in the *Guardian* (12 September 1995) entitled 'What a mess to clear up!', reporting the launch of the SCAA Preschool Education consultation document, began like this: 'The hordes of four year olds piling into nurseries and playgroups this week are far too busy with the paint and glue and sand and water to worry about the mess they are causing. But Gillian Shepherd has a lot of clearing up to do.'

They, the children, have caused no *mess* at all, but this characterization of children as the *problem* is an important one to note. That same article forecast a fierce debate between progressives and traditionalists. Well, perhaps this is one situation where we can confidently say that traditional nursery education *is* progressive. The traditions of learning through play and observation of children begun and developed by the Macmillans and Isaacs are the very strands of nursery education which are now being cast as *child-centred* and *progressive*.

This book represents a hope for further progression in the development of educational provision for young children. The contributors highlight what is good in current traditions. They discuss the place of, and progress in, children's rights through topics including: inspection; equality; curriculum, observation and assessment; special educational needs; training early childhood workers; work with parents; and play. The final chapter discusses one article of the UN Convention posing a series of questions for educators to debate in relation to their own work with children. I hope that those who read *Respectful Educators – Capable Learners* will look forward to how things might be if, as individuals and as a nation, we further take account of the need to respect children, their capabilities and their rights and help them to reach their potential.

Cathy Nutbrown
January 1996

Perhaps what one wants to say is formed in childhood and the rest of one's life is spent in trying to say it.

Barbara Hepworth

Educaré . . . to cherish the growth of the young.

Christian Schiller

The well being of children requires political action at the highest level. We are determined to take that action. We ourselves make a solemn commitment to give high priority to the rights of children.

Seventy-one heads of state and government
World Summit for Children, New York, September 1990

respe'ct
> pay heed to; relate to, be directed to or concerned with. Regard with deference, esteem, or honour; avoid degrading or insulting or injuring or interfering with or interrupting, treat with consideration, spare, refrain from offending or corrupting . . .

respe'ctful
> showing deference . . .

respe'cting
> having reference to . . .

ca'pable
> having the ability or fitness for . . .
> gifted, able, competent

ca'pability
> Power of . . . power for . . . power to . . .

1

The United Nations Convention on the Rights of the Child – Progress in the United Kingdom

Gerison Lansdown

In December 1991 the UK government ratified the UN Convention on the Rights of the Child. It was a potentially momentous occasion. For the first time ever, an explicit commitment, binding under international law, was being made to respect children's socio-cultural as well as civil rights. The Convention was drafted over a ten-year period from 1979–89 and adopted by the UN General Assembly in November 1989. It addresses children's rights in every sphere of their lives – rights to protection, to freedom from discrimination, to survival and development, to security and family life, to participation in all matters of concern to them. It now has the support of almost every country in the world, a record unprecedented in the history of the UN. No other international human rights treaty has attracted a comparable level of support. Ratification imposes a number of significant obligations on the government. Firstly, and most obviously, there is an obligation to ensure that the principles contained in the Convention are respected for all children. Article 4 requires governments to implement the rights to the maximum extent possible. Secondly, the government is required to ensure that the Convention is publicized and that adults and children are aware of its provisions. Thirdly, there is a requirement after two years and subsequently every five years to produce a report to the UN Committee on the Rights of the Child, the international body established to monitor the Convention, on its progress towards implementation. The Committee has produced guidelines for governments producing reports. These guidelines state that the process of producing the report should be one that 'encourages and facilitates popular participation and public scrutiny of government policies'. They suggest that the process should be used as an opportunity for 'conducting a comprehensive review of the various measures undertaken to harmonise national law and policy with the Convention', (Centre for Human Rights, 1991).

The UK's first report was due in January 1994 and was in fact published and submitted to the Committee in February of that year (HMSO, 1994). Despite the Committee's guidelines, there had been no consultation prior to its publication and certainly no public review of the measures needed to ensure compliance. Indeed, it was a report which failed to acknowledge that there was any aspect of legislation, policy or practice in the UK which needed change, improvement, reconsideration, better monitoring or better resourcing.

The Committee recognizes that governments will not always present a self-critical or comprehensive commentary of the state of children's rights in their country. They have therefore encouraged non-governmental organizations to present alternative reports providing a differing perspective on the implementation of the rights in the Convention. In the UK the Children's Rights Development Unit, a short-term independent charity with the support of all the key child welfare organizations, was created to undertake this work. By working collaboratively with organizations in the voluntary, statutory, professional and academic fields, the Unit produced an alternative report which presented an altogether more critical analysis of the extent to which the principles and standards in the Convention were being met. This report, the *UK Agenda for Children* (Lansdown and Newell, 1994), was also submitted to the UN Committee.,

When the Committee met in January 1995 to examine the UK government delegation, it had therefore received two documents drawing very different pictures of what was happening to children in the UK. Clearly, in many respects, we would already appear to meet the standards imposed by the Convention. We have free universal education at primary and secondary levels, free health care, a Children Act rooted in principles of the paramountcy of the child's welfare, and right to family life. We have legislation rendering discrimination on the basis of sex or race unlawful. Children, in general, are treated separately from adults in the criminal justice system, special provision exists for the education and care of children with disabilities or special needs, and considerable effort has been invested in seeking to create effective child-protection procedures. So, despite the critical report produced by the Children's Rights Development Unit, it was with some confidence that the UK government presented itself to the Committee.

However, after two days of rigorous questioning of the delegation, the Committee produced concluding observations which were extremely critical of many aspects of government policy. While the members positively endorsed a number of government initiatives, including the Children Act and the Code of Practice on Special Educational Needs, they also expressed a number of very significant concerns in relation to both substantive rights contained in the Convention and the lack of procedures established by the government to achieve effective implementation.

Article 4 of the Convention places an obligation on governments to designate resources to the promotion of socio-economic and cultural rights to the 'maximum extent possible'. Article 27 provides that children have the right to a standard of living adequate for their proper development. But the Committee was concerned about the high and growing numbers of children living in poverty, with all the consequent implications for their health and life chances, about the evidence of the very considerable growth in inequality in the UK between rich and poor – now greater than at any time since the nineteenth century – the growing phenomenon of young people sleeping and begging on the streets and the withdrawal of income support to 16–17-year-olds.

The Committee paid particular attention to the extent of violence perpetrated against children. The members were deeply concerned by evidence they had received which demonstrated that the legislation permitting 'reasonable chastisement' of children allowed levels of violence which were clearly in breach of article 19: the right to protection from all forms of physical and mental violence. They questioned the apparent inconsistency in the position of the government, which had stated in its report to the Committee that 'physical punishment has no place in the child care environment', with the recently published guidance from the Department of Health endorsing the right of childminders to smack children in their care as long as they had the parents' permission. Indeed, they were not satisfied with the response of the delegation that the government considered the issue of physical punishment to be a private matter to be decided by parents. They argued forcefully that the right of children to protection from all forms of physical violence was a fundamental human right from which the government could not abdicate its responsibility in favour of parental choice. Physical punishment of any kind was inconsistent with article 19. Indeed, one member of the UN Committee observed that 'the UK position represented a vestige of the outdated view that children were in a sense their parents' chattel' (Committee on the Rights of the Child 1995). The Committee also questioned the failure of the government to extend the right of children to protection from corporal punishment in state schools to those children whose parents pay for them to be educated. And it expressed concern about the lack of family support and parent education.

The Committee members were disturbed by the evidence that children can be excluded from school with no right in law to be given an opportunity to defend themselves, and also that the unilateral right of parents to withdraw children from sex and religious education was not consistent with the obligation to take account of the views and wishes of children and indeed their right to information. They argued that procedures needed to be introduced to ensure that children are provided with the opportunity to express their views on matters of concern to them in the running of schools and recommended that the training curriculum of teachers should incorporate education about the Convention on the Rights of the Child and that teaching methods should be inspired by and reflect its spirit and philosophy (see chapters 4 and 7). They also considered that the best interests of the child needed to be explicitly reflected in education, health and social security legislation.

The Committee took the view that the age of criminal responsibility which currently stands at 10 (8 in Scotland) is too low to reflect the spirit of the Convention and in particular article 3, the duty to ensure that the best interests of the child are always a primary consideration. But it was the provisions of the Criminal Justice and Public Order Act 1994 which gave greatest cause for concern, given that this legislation, which introduces secure training centres for 12–14-year-olds, and extends sentencing for young offenders, breaches the obligations to use imprisonment only as a measure of last resort and for the shortest appropriate period of time and yet has been brought in since the government ratified the Convention.

The Committee also took the view that there was a need for an independent body to monitor implementation of the Convention, in the form of a children's commissioner or ombudsman.

The government and indeed much of the media were outraged at this explicit criticism of the record of the UK in an international arena. They felt unjustly accused given the poor record of respecting children which pertains in so many other countries in the world. But it is in this reaction that it becomes clear that the government has underestimated the nature of the Convention and its purpose.

The Convention provides a framework of principles and standards to serve as an aspiration for governments. For example, it is not good enough in the UK to respond to article 28 – the right to free education on the basis of equality of opportunity – simply by asserting that the Education Act 1944 provides for free education for all children. The Convention demands a more rigorous investigation of the application of that legislation. Is this right being fulfilled for the growing numbers of children being excluded from school? Is the education of children from multiply deprived backgrounds being offered on the basis of equality of opportunity when the state offers little or no early years provision which could mitigate much of the disadvantage those children experience? Is the continuing number of disabled children, who are being educated in special schools and denied opportunities for inclusive education, consistent with a policy of equality of opportunity (see chapter 6)? Similarly, the health service is free at the point of delivery for all and would therefore appear to comply with the requirement in article 24 that children are entitled to the best possible health care and have the right to life. But is it good enough when a child born to a family in a poor working-class family is twice as likely to die as a child born to professional parents or when children with unemployed parents are twelve times more likely to be killed in road accidents as children in professional families, when children from deprived families suffer from consistently poorer health (OPCS/HMSO, 1989; Kumar, 1993)

Is the principle contained in article 12, that all children have the right to express a view on all matters of concern to them and to have that view taken seriously, really complied with in family life, in education, in health care, in the development of services for children? The Children Act 1989 requires courts and local authorities to ascertain the wishes and feelings of children when making decisions concerning their welfare. And the government placed great emphasis on these provisions in its presentation to the UN Committee. But the Children Act affects only a very limited number of children in a very limited area of their lives. The obligation to listen to children will arise only at a point of crisis – breakdown of marriage, or coming into the care of the local authority. But is article 12 being adequately respected when no such obligation extends to parents, or to schools, and it is within the family and schools that children spend most of their time and where it is of primary importance that children learn that their opinions and feelings will be respected and valued?

The answer to all these questions has to be 'no' and it is the government's failure even to begin to *ask* those questions that led to the Committee producing such a searing critique of the implementation of the Convention in the UK. We were not being compared with developing countries with gross national products infinitely smaller than our own. The purpose of monitoring implementation is not to produce a league table of comparative progress. It is to explore how well countries are doing given their resources, political situation, history, stability and culture. No country will or could fully comply with all the provisions of the Convention. It represents a set of goals to focus and inspire policy development. What the Committee is seeking is an indication from governments that they have undertaken that commitment. It found it lacking in the UK.

But the way forward is not unproblematic. It is not only the government which is resistant to an explicit promotion of children's rights. Children's rights are generally viewed with some hostility in the UK – associated with aggressive, demanding and badly behaved adolescents out of the control of their parents and teachers and lacking the willingness or capacity to accept the responsibilities that should accompany the granting of rights. This hostility appears to be rooted in fear – fear of loss of control, loss of authority, loss of respect and loss of status. And it also appears that it is the very language of rights that promotes the fear. It is therefore important to examine in some detail what is meant by children's rights, what rights children have and the implications of those rights, because in fact most adults would accept without question a range of fundamental rights as applied to children.

There would be little disagreement, for example, that children have the right to life, to the best possible health, to free education on the basis of equality of opportunity, to play and recreation, to freedom from discrimination, to a standard of living adequate for their proper development. In other words, children's rights to survival and development are uncontentious. There will always be disagreement over the level of provision necessary to fulfil the obligations to children associated with those rights but the principle itself is not in question. Similarly, in the field of children's rights to protection, there would be general agreement that children have the right to protection from sexual exploitation, from abduction and from violence and abuse. Again there might be considerable dispute over the nature of protection necessary and, indeed, what constitutes violence in respect of children – for example, smacking not being considered as violence by the majority of the population – but the principle that children are entitled to protection from a range of experiences that could be harmful to them is not challenged.

Acceptance of the legitimacy of these rights derives from a view of childhood in which the child is seen as the rightful recipient of the adults' protective care and responsibility. It constructs parenthood as a set of obligations which at the same time confers certain rights and from which the child is intended to benefit. And although the fulfilment of those obligations imposed by recognition of the child's rights might at times be demanding, difficult or onerous, the obligations themselves do not in any way threaten the status of the parent. Indeed it is because the child has those rights that the parents acquire rights themselves. The right of the parent to consent to treatment of a child, to change its name, to determine where it lives, which school it goes to, to punish it, all derive from implicit assumptions about the child's right to care, protection and guidance. In other words, these rights do not undermine the rights of the parent. On the contrary, they are the very source of the parent's authority in relation to the child.

However, when one moves into the arena of children's civil rights which require that adults' relationships with children become not only those of protector, provider or advocate but also negotiator, facilitator or observer, the willingness to accept the legitimacy of the rights is far less widespread. As soon as it is proposed that children not only have a right to express a view on matters of concern to them but must also be taken seriously, then the power of parents to exercise choices and make decisions in relation to the child is necessarily diminished. Not surprisingly then, it is in this area that the antipathy to the concept of rights for children is most pronounced. But these rights in the Convention – to participate, to freedom of expression, religion, conscience, information, to privacy – are given equal status with all other rights.

Children's views are still, for a substantial proportion of the adult population, variously considered to be ill-informed, irrational, irresponsible, amusing or cute. It is much more unusual for them to be given serious recognition and, then, primarily when their views coincide with those of adults. The old adage 'children should be seen and not heard' still tends to hold surprising sway. Suggestions that greater recognition should be given to children's views have been greeted with a vehement backlash of public opinion claiming that children already have too many rights.

A number of arguments are promulgated in defence of opposing civil rights for children:

(1) *Children cannot have rights until they are capable of exercising responsibility.* It can be argued that the right of a child to be consulted on matters of concern to him or her imposes responsibilities on adults to ensure that the child has sufficient information with which to participate in contributing to the making of informed choices and that the opportunities are available in which to take part in any decision-making processes. But clearly it also imposes obligations on children to ensure that the right is respected for others. And it is the very process of being consulted, and involved in decisions that affect their lives, that will enable children to begin to develop the skills and understanding to understand the implications of those decisions and their impact on others. A child who is told to listen to and respect others while feeling that no reciprocal obligation applies to her or him, is likely to resent and reject the injunction. But a child whose opinions are listened to, who is given information and explanations, and who is encouraged to articulate views is learning the skills associated with social responsibility and is far more likely to understand that those rights carry obligations towards others.

(2) *Children are not competent to participate in decision-making.* Much of the concern about recognizing a child's right to participate in decision-making derives from a failure to distinguish between participation and autonomy or self-determination. Participation is a process of recognizing that children are players in their own lives, that they have views and experiences which can contribute to effective decision-making, and that they must be involved in such decisions. Article 12, the right of children to express a view on all matters of concern to them and to have that view taken seriously, clearly insists on respect for this right. However, it qualifies the exercise of choice for children by stating that 'the views of the child shall be given due weight in accordance with the age and maturity of the child'. In other words, it does not grant the child autonomy. Respect for the child's right to participate is not the same as granting the child autonomy. Autonomy, which allows the child the right to determine decision-making, must necessarily be bounded by assessments of the child's competence and understanding of the choices available to her or him and the implications of those decisions.

Adults do have clear responsibilities for the protection and welfare of children. A parent must make an infinite number of decisions and judgements every day in respect of a child. The Convention on the Rights of the Child acknowledges this responsibility in article 5, which states that governments must 'respect the responsibilities, rights and duties of parents . . . to provide . . . appropriate direction and guidance in the exercise by the child of the rights [in the Convention]'. However, it also recognizes boundaries in the exercise of those responsibilities by asserting that they must be carried out 'in a manner consistent with the child's evolving capacity'. In other words, adults do not have unfettered rights to act on children's behalf. The Convention places further constraints on the powers of adults with responsibility for children by requiring, in article 3, that 'In all actions concerning children, whether undertaken by public or private social welfare institutions, courts of law, administrative authorities or legislative bodies, the best interests of the child shall be a primary consideration.' These obligations taken together require of parents that they promote opportunities for the child to participate as a route towards increased autonomy while also ensuring that the child is adequately protected from harm.

(3) *Rights for children threaten the stability and harmony of family life.* The recognition that children have the right to participate in decisions that affect them does cut across traditional notions of the power of parents to exercise complete control over their children's lives. It does necessarily involve a greater emphasis on negotiation, compromise and sharing of information. These processes imply a more democratic model of family life and are certainly not irreconcilable with cohesion and stability within families. On the contrary, mutual respect for all family members is likely to promote a greater capacity for long-term friendships and affection. Democratic decision-making processes are more time-consuming and can be frustrating and difficult to maintain at times but the long-term benefits will be the creation of an environment in which children have the optimum opportunity to gain in both the confidence and the capacity to participate as socially responsible individuals.

(4) *The imposition of rights takes away children's opportunities for childhood.* It is often argued that the imposition of responsibilities on children denies them the opportunity for childhood. However, article 12 does not imply any obligation on children to participate in decision-making, merely that any child willing to express a view has a right to do so and that children capable of understanding the implications of an action have the right to exercise a choice. For many adults, childhood is imbued with a rather romanticized notion of innocence – a period free from responsibility or conflict and dominated by fantasy, play and opportunity. Attempts to offer children greater control over their lives is seen as an intrusion into this period, denying them the right to enjoy their childhood. But for many children childhood is experienced as a period characterized by powerlessness and a lack of control over what happens to them. One of the most frequent reasons cited by children for wanting to grow up is the desire to be able to exercise more control over their lives.

During a consultation exercise undertaken by the Children's Rights Development Unit in 1993, forty-five groups of children aged 5–18 years were approached to discuss their perceptions of how their rights were respected (Lansdown and Newell, 1994). The children came from a wide variety of life experiences but common to all groups was a powerful sense of frustration that their views and experiences were not taken seriously at home, at school, by politicians, by policy-makers and the media.

There is a long way to go before we can claim that our respect for children's rights is consistent with the demands placed upon us by the Convention. There is a great deal that the government needs to address within legislation but also in setting a public agenda of active commitment to implementation. But the obligations do not rest with the government alone. Everyone involved with children, professionally and personally, needs to examine their policies and practice against the principles and standards of the Convention. As a starting point this can be done by asking the following questions:

- Are children being encouraged and enabled from the earliest appropriate age to take decisions for themselves? Examples include choice of activities, friendships, what they wear.
- Are children's views given serious consideration and properly respected? Or are they dismissed, trivialized or discounted? For example, is there any opportunity for children to contribute to the policy of the school or play centre? Some primary schools now have pupil councils in which children can contribute to the development of behaviour policies, school rules, the use of the playground.
- Is children's privacy respected? Or are communications or even confidences from children shared indiscriminately among adults? Many adults recount children's stories as entertainment for one another without thought for the right of the child to respect for her or his privacy.
- Is the same courtesy when listening to adults extended to children? For example, it is often seen as unacceptable for a child to interrupt an adult but the child can be and frequently is interrupted by adults. The lesson children learn is that their conversation is less valuable than that of adults.
- Is children's right to physical integrity respected, with full recognition that all forms of physical punishment and deliberate humiliation are degrading and hurtful?
- Are children provided with information and guidance to help them develop their own opinions and beliefs without undue influence being exerted by adults?

The Convention on the Rights of the Child provides us with an exciting challenge. It proposes a radical shift in the status of children in society and in the structure of relationships between adults and children. These changes necessitate a re-evaluation of many of our traditional assumptions and practices in child care, education, play and family life. But renegotiation does not imply the dismantling of all that is positive for children and parents within the family. It does not in any way threaten the importance or value of children's relationships with adults. Indeed one member of the UN Committee on the Rights of the Child, Marta Santos Pais, has observed: 'The rights of the family can only be envisaged alongside respect for rights of individual members. Diversity cannot in any way threaten the harmony and unity of the family, rather it decisively reinforces its democratic structure, while strengthening ties of affection, confidence and trust' (Children's Rights Office, 1995, p. 3). The Convention provides the basic tools for analysing and evaluating practice. The task is now in the hands of every adult living or working with children to translate those tools into fundamental changes in the reality of children's lives.

2

Inspection of Early Years in Schools

Jean Ensing

'Improvement through inspection'[1]

Inspection, done properly, matters because its goal is to improve schools: first by informing parents, professionals, public and politicians about the quality of education provided in them and, secondly, by promoting school development after the inspection. The intention 'Improvement through inspection' is the same for all schools, whether the children are aged 3–5, or of statutory age 5+–16. The schools with the youngest children receive the same entitlement to an inspection process that looks at standards of achievement, the quality of education, the efficiency of the school and the children's spiritual, moral, social and cultural development.

By securing the same inspection focus for young children, their education is awarded the same degree of professional and public regard. Young children's right to education is recognized and enhanced by the requirement that it should be of good quality. Inspection therefore commits the education system and the government to protect and care for children. It advocates high quality schooling for them and thus supports a main principle in the UN Convention – of paying attention to the needs of children.

This position is, however, changing because of the government's latest initiative for expanding nursery education through giving parents vouchers (DFEE, 1996). The idea is to take money away from maintained schools (where education is free) and give it to parents to spend for part of either a free or a fee-paying place. Whatever type of 'other' nursery place is bought, it will be inspected. A new 'light touch' type of inspection was promised (DFEE, 1995). Too light a touch, that is, of minimal requirements, may lead to minimal quality provision and that would reduce children's rights. This is a real risk because the 'voucher' idea coincides with the proposed removal or reduction of building regulation requirements (DFE, 1989) which at present ensure adequate space and facilities in schools. More nursery education could equal more cheap and inferior education.

All forms of inspection are struggling to keep up with the demands. No inspection teams made bids for a third of the schools in the first primary round. Many local authorities who inspect other forms of non-school provision, for children under 8 years old, are still trying to clear the backlog of inspection required under the Children Act. In some cases resources exist only to enable inspectors to enforce minimal safety requirements rather than improve the quality of provision. Light-touch inspections may be economic possibilities but such a system is unlikely to support children's rights.

At present and very importantly the early years of schooling are not demeaned by a lesser form of inspection. All schools, regardless of type, have their turn in an open inspection process. This positive aspect is countered, however, by a major drawback: the nature of the statutory inspection process is more suited to the ways secondary schools, and secondary school inspectors, work.

Developing inspection

The development of inspection has been a long and mostly gradual process. For some 150 years Her Majesty's Inspectors (HMI) have been monitoring the schooling system at a national level, as an independent arm of government. Sometimes what HMI said proved uncomfortable but their reports stimulated professional debate. An example is the seminal quote from Katharine Bathurst, HMI, who looked at young children in elementary schools in 1905 and said: 'There is much to stifle curiosity and dull the mind.'

Her report prompted the development of 'infant' education, i.e. schooling that paid attention to the needs of the youngest children. The HMI's publication in 1989 of *The Education of Children Under Five* pointed out that children in nursery schools and classes usually received a better quality education than those in primary classes. This strengthened the case both for improving the provision in reception classes and for increasing designated nursery education. Although central government did not take up these issues local government did. Local education authorities (LEAs) had built up regular monitoring (accompanied by advice and support) of the schools in their localities. This was done by teams of local advisers and inspectors (LAI) and included versions of self-evaluation by schools and reviews or inspections by LAI.

In the late 1980s an exciting development was the pilot joint-inspection arrangement between HMI and seven LEAs. Those involved, from each group, thought that this way of joint working could be the model for extensive and regular high quality inspection of schools. Alone,

HMI could not provide sufficiently frequent inspections and, alone, LAI could not provide a commonly accepted and nationally credible model of inspection. Joint working allowed HMI to combine a national perspective with the detailed local knowledge of LAI. Joint working, however, was not popular with ministers who wanted inspectors to be drawn from outside education. It ceased after the pilot. Those involved in the pilot argued that the ending of this project was not in the best interests of schools or inspectors.

Outside inspection – by OFSTED inspectors

In 1992 there was a new Schools Act (HMG, 1992) that legislated for schools to be inspected every four years. The Act did not define the inspection process but passed that responsibility to the new office of Her Majesty's Chief Inspector (HMCI). At the same time the existing HMI in England were incorporated into a new government department, led by HMCI, called the Office for Standards in Education (OFSTED). The first tasks for HMI were to:

- develop criteria for inspection which met the requirements in the Education Act (these criteria are known as the 'Framework');
- write a handbook for inspection, with extensive guidance for interpreting the Framework;
- train inspectors to carry out the inspections.

Within a year, a short space of time, many thought too short for sufficient consultation, the first two of these tasks were accomplished. The consultation paid some attention to the views of lay people and educationists. It did not take account of children's views about what children wanted or felt about their education – in either the spirit of the Children Act or the letter of the UN Convention. In September 1993 the new inspection process for secondary schools began, followed a year later by primary (including nursery) schools. Schools no longer talked about being inspected – the verb 'to be OFSTEDED' entered education jargon!

The OFSTED Framework refreshingly opened up the criteria for inspection. The insiders – teachers and school governors, the LEAs supporting schools, teacher trainers, the teacher associations and unions – knew explicitly what was being inspected. Outsiders also saw what inspectors were looking for. OFSTED set out, through the *Handbook* (OFSTED, 1993), ways inspectors should look at, discuss and judge what schools, teachers and children do. The opening up of inspection was welcomed by everyone involved but alongside the welcome went a shiver of fear. Schools and inspectors, particularly in the primary and nursery stages, wondered how they could meet all the requirements of the Framework as exemplified in great detail in the *Handbook*.

Fear and concerns

A number of attacks and perceived threats fed the fears. For a start the media proclaimed that inspection would weed out the weak schools and relished the idea of considerable publicity for the 'failing schools'. Even the most effective schools and the most conscientious teachers feared being labelled failures because of the great number of inspection criteria they had to meet. That fear was fuelled by those who blamed 'progressive' and 'trendy' methods in schools for a claimed decline in standards of achievement and behaviour. These assertions were often illustrated by comparing primary with secondary classrooms. So, for example, rows of children silently listening to a teacher were a 'traditional' learning organization proclaimed as correct. By contrast, a 'progressive' organization in which children learned independently, made choices, engaged in different activities, moved around and at times worked in groups was declared disastrous. Yet primary and nursery teachers knew that the latter form of basic and active learning was that successfully used with 3–5-year-olds. The pronouncements censuring schools treated in the same way the teaching methods and classroom organizations schools used, whether the children were aged 3 or 13. Most of those who spoke, wrote or were interviewed avoided the distinction between what was appropriate, i.e. traditional, and successful for children of 4 and those of 14 years. The tendency to blame schools for educational and social failure and to associate these factors with the criticism of teaching methods preceded and arguably peaked with the start of the inspection process. While many educationists accepted that it was healthy to debate the teaching of older junior-age children (8–11) most felt that in the early years schools needed, and in the main had, a developmentally appropriate curriculum – a curriculum that worked in the best interests of young children.

Early years practitioners feared that the OFSTED model for inspection concentrated unduly on the subject-specific National Curriculum; that the inspection of separate subjects undermined the methods used extensively in early years education. Schools felt under pressure to provide a curriculum better suited to older children. The curriculum muddle was exacerbated by the ambiguous guidance about the National Curriculum starting point. To put it simply, schools were unclear when and how to begin teaching the National Curriculum. As an entitlement curriculum it did not make sense for the National Curriculum to span six, seven, eight or nine terms depending on the age of admission. Any difference in time-span disenfranchised the child who began school at statutory age and so was unfair. Also the idea of taking up to three years to teach and to learn what could or should take only two years was illogical and inefficient. Teachers struggled with their professional knowledge: knowledge that young children need a curriculum that takes account of their particular stages of development rather than a curriculum that seeks to fit them into a ten-subject straitjacket. In short the teachers felt they knew best what worked for the 3-, 4- and young 5-year-olds but they feared that their best did not fit with the Framework for inspection.

In fact OFSTED supported good early years practice and tried to promote the developmental curriculum by issuing guidance, in the *Handbook*, on inspecting early years classes (OFSTED, 1993). However, the guidance, while welcomed by teachers and inspectors, did not fit well with the inspection process. For example, to allow inspectors to track the different subjects in classrooms means that schools have to produce strict timetables. This is fine in the secondary school but problematic in a nursery or reception class. There is one type of lesson-observation form for all age groups. It has to be coded in National Curriculum subjects irrespective of the labels the school or the technical paper uses. Grades for each area of learning are counted notwithstanding that in a group of 3–5-year-olds the grades might apply to only a handful of children. Brave inspectors treat the paperwork flexibly and with caution, others fear the censure of the OFSTED monitors and spend an inordinate amount of time gathering the missing 'evidence'; that further pressures the schools and themselves.

The difference between inspecting primary and secondary schools is stark. A secondary school will commonly have twelve or more inspectors. Each deals with one subject plus possibly an *aspect* of inspection such as equality of opportunity over a period of three to five days. On a small primary/nursery inspection two inspectors may each have to cover up to five subjects plus 5 *aspects* in two days. The secondary inspector has to write one or two sections of the report while the primary inspector has to write up to ten. Overall the primary inspector in a small school has to do five times the work in half the time. The secondary teacher is observed much less than the primary/nursery teacher. An additional factor in early years classes is that children are often managed (taught) by nursery nurses, teaching assistants or volunteer parents. Some of these adults may have a qualification to work with children but the judgements made of all of them contribute to the evaluation of the quality of teaching in the school.

Schools also fear that the inspectors of the children aged 3–5 years lack credibility. A substantial majority of inspectors have a secondary background and few have experience of working with young children. The spectre of secondary inspectors with a background of expertise in one subject inspecting the whole curriculum in a nursery or reception class astonishes schools. People working with 3–5-year-old children continuously observe their responses to assess their stages of development and varying levels of competence. Schools wonder how inspectors without that background and expertise can judge children's standards of achievement and the quality of their learning and of the adults' teaching.

In my experience the inspectors without early years expertise tend to overestimate the quality they see. They are impressed by the way young children respond positively to any form of activity; by the high level of interest and motivation young children display; by the characteristic warmth of relationships between young children and the adults who work with them. These features contrast with the sometimes cynical lack of interest of the older pupil and tend, therefore, to mask the effectiveness of the teaching and learning. Expertise and relevant experience are important for inspector and inspected. It will benefit no one if inspection suffers, by being too soft or too hard, because the assessors and the assessed do not know and trust each other.

Inspection – costs and benefits

Schools know that they are on the list for inspection up to twelve months in advance. Such knowledge can be a benefit or a cost. The preparation for inspection can be very positive. The school may audit and assess the quality of teaching, learning, resources and support systems. Staff may use the *Handbook* as part of their professional development: to check their responsibilities and performance against the criteria for inspection. Portfolios of children's work may be upgraded to provide evidence for those parts of the curriculum that may not be seen during the inspection. In short, the school continues, with added focus and some urgency, its own form of monitoring. Its self-evaluation contributes to its professional development. This protects the moral and professional framework of children's rights by securing a full and appropriate teaching and learning programme for children.

Some schools use the waiting period less constructively, sometimes destructively. They may seek to defend expected criticism with a mountain of paperwork. This places a great burden on staff. They focus on writing up policy and guidance and are diverted from the proper assessment of what children do, how they learn, and how staff teach. Some teachers suffer unduly from anxiety. They cancel holidays and may spend a disproportionate amount of time making their classrooms attractive. In short, the school's energies may be deflected into trying to jump the perceived inspection hurdles rather than tackling any weaknesses.

Such negative responses trap schools and commit them merely to presenting or maintaining rather than developing practice and expertise. At the extreme, negative preparation is a form of educational neglect from which children ought to be protected. Fortunately, extreme examples are rare but aspects of them and myths about them pervade the system and add to the stress schools feel.

The inspectors also prepare for inspection. Before the inspection the Registered Inspector visits the school to meet staff, governors and parents. The team of inspectors write the pre-inspection sections in the Record of Inspection Evidence. This is based on documents provided by the school, the information from OFSTED in the Pre-Inspection Context and School

Indicator (PICSI) report and the preliminary visits. Although OFSTED wants concise notes that are intended to brief the inspection team, in practice inspectors write too much under the fifteen pre-inspection commentary sections. In the main, they do so to 'pass' the OFSTED monitoring procedure. A number of dangers arise from this part of inspection.

A good school might have poor paperwork and a weak school glossy, well-produced documents. The complexity of managing, organizing and guiding school practice is hard to represent in written text. The primary school PICSI reports, from OFSTED, have little practical use. The material is often months out of date. Since the circumstances of primary schools can change markedly from term to term any analysis needs to be so qualified as to be useless. But at the pre-inspection stage inspectors are required to set out 'Key issues for inspection' based on hypotheses made largely on the paperwork supplied. Any issues raised have then to be answered from inspection evidence. Identifying too many issues based on paperwork wastes inspectors' time. It may also lead to weak hypotheses that during the inspection divert energy from the real purpose. That is, to find out how well the school staff translate policy, written or unwritten, into practice and implement the school's plans for the benefit of teaching and learning.

Connecting judgement and improvement

School inspection must report on standards, quality, efficiency and ethos. How does that essential focus on outcomes help school improvement and therefore act in the best interests of the child?

Standards

Parents often ask what 'standards' mean. They know what a standard measure is (gallon or mile but probably not a litre or centimetre like their children). Parents know they like the standard of behaviour in the school but they do not know what the standard of English should be at 40 or 50 months of age. Giving parents an answer is not easy because we use 'standards' in two ways: first, as a description of a level reached and, secondly, as a judgement of the quality of the level attained.

Judging the standards as levels achieved, by children aged between 36 and 60 months, is like walking in a minefield! The difficulty is not new. Schools and inspectors have always judged whether a child is responding typically for the age range but have tended to talk of competence. Looking at competence is effective; nursery schools have a good record for identifying very early the children with special educational needs. But inspectors have to judge standards as 'progress' or 'gains'. The idea of 'value-added' by the school is hard to measure. Any form of assessment at the point of entry to school, at best based on observation of the child engaged in exploratory play and interaction with other children and adults, may reveal snapshots of the child's developing skills, attitudes and knowledge. At entry one 3-year-old may be able to sort toy animals by colour, another child by colour and size. Six months later both can sort by colour, size and habitat. Is the first child making more rapid progress? If so what affected it? Was it the nursery visit to the farm, handling the snake brought in by a parent or the documentaries on television? Was it a combination of the three? Was it the failure of the initial observation to identify what the child already knew but could not express?

Judging standards as the quality of level attained, i.e. whether attainment is appropriate, is like walking in a minefield wearing a blindfold. Young children develop at different rates physically, socially, intellectually, emotionally and linguistically. Unlike the relatively mature 7–16-year-olds, the 3–5-year-old child can make great gains in one area in a short space of time.

In the early years it is difficult and probably futile to try to sum up the magic of learning into 'standards' whether as 'levels' or 'quality' of attainment. Measuring standards is not as simple as measuring medicine. Nor is assessing 'value-added' simple when you cannot be sure about the starting point. Besides, adults who work with young children know that levels of attainment are imperfect as indicators of later success. History gives many examples of the 'late developer' who goes on to be a genius or the 'early developer' who fizzles out. In part, OFSTED recognizes these difficulties in the general and broad way it outlines the criteria for reporting on standards for young children (OFSTED, 1993). But that recognition is countered by the rigidity of the inspection and monitoring procedures. Inspectors of early years settings, held to the requirement to report on standards globally, are having to jump a hurdle set for the secondary phase where standards are measured by examinations and tests.

Young children are highly individual. They develop at their own pace. Generally they are active, curious and live in the present. But they are also driven by their own overwhelming interests as they seek to make sense of their world. The children driven by the goal of mastering writing their names will do so not only with pencil but with painting, in clay, sand and water, with dough and on a chalkboard. The child intent on understanding the idea of circles will draw, use string, rail and road tracks, large and small blocks to make enclosures; sit inside circles of equipment; run, jump and cycle in circles. In the nursery environment between 25 and 120 children will be pursuing, for a good part of the session, their own learning agenda. With the support and approval of adults they will be exercising their independence in learning.

At the very least it is expecting a great deal of inspectors to simplify all those elements of achievement into a simple global statement – 'the standards achieved are . . .'. Where there is any doubt children must be given the benefit of that doubt. And how can there by anything but doubt where young children are concerned? The requirement to report on standards as though it is straightforward and simple flies in the face of article 29 – 'schools should help children develop their skills and personality fully' – because it cannot do justice to the fullness of children's development. It cannot be in the best interests of children to beat schools with a stick called 'standards' when a 'standard' 3- or 4-year-old has such a wide range of competence.

Quality

The quality of education is a mixture of everything that happens in a school. It has many features including the quality of learning and teaching. Here inspection is on much firmer ground since the heart of education concerns learning and teaching. Judging their quality also means analysing the way they are supported by staff, resources, relationships, environment, leadership and partnership with parents and governors.

Evidence, however, has to be collected in a secure and objective way. OFSTED rightly requires that inspectors do this mainly by observation. Checklists to measure quantities of resources, space, staff, policies; interviews to detail management structures, curriculum planning and assessment, links with parents and other agencies provide only a back-cloth to the quality of provision. Observations of teachers teaching and children learning, however, are recorded on lesson-observation forms. The same type of form has to be used whether the pupils are aged 13 and in a science lesson or aged 3 in the nursery school garden! The 13-year-olds are all different but they are likely to be engaged on the same experiment, using the same equipment, reading the same text in a lesson lasting 45 or 90 minutes with a specialist teacher. That is, at least, the assumption and the inspector will complete one form. The 3-year-olds may be engaged in one of fifteen different activities, lasting from 30 seconds to 30 minutes and involving teachers, nursery nurses, support assistants and parent volunteers. The children may be looking at books under a tree, watching snails, digging in the sand, pouring water into containers, planting seedlings, climbing on apparatus, pushing, pulling and riding vehicles. The inspector must observe, evaluate and record either a single activity or a strand through a range of experiences. This does not fit comfortably with completing one or many forms. It is a simplistic notion that inspectors operate in the same way with young children and mature students. No wonder inspectors are reluctant to inspect early years and so many small school inspection contracts are left without takers. This is not in the best interests of young children especially those in small schools.

Efficiency

OFSTED wants to know if schools give 'value for money'. The focus is, on one hand, evaluating the 'outcomes of the school in relation to its use of resources' (OFSTED, 1993). On the other hand, the *Handbook* – Technical Paper and Subsequent Guidance requires inspectors to judge 'whether there are sufficient resources used to optimum effect for young children' (OFSTED, 1993). No primary school I have ever visited has complained of too much cash or wondered how to spend its money. Of course mistakes are made in early years economies but they are minute compared to the spending of the secondary school. A tiny sum will of course be a big proportion of a small budget but we all know that percentages are not always proper comparisons – think of comparing percentage increases for the lowly and the highly paid.

The public as consumers know that 'you get what you pay for'. Unit costs for the youngest children are high simply because of paying the number of necessary adults. Even so the unit cost for those on the lowest rung of education is lower than for those on the top rung. Educating all abilities at 4 is deemed to cost less than educating the highest ability at 18. At both these ages full-time maintained education is non-compulsory and at present free. What we evaluate is only whether the available funds, sufficient or not, are spent efficiently. The inspection process does not ask the essential question – what would be the real cost of high quality early years education? Now that *would* be in the best interests of children.

Spiritual, moral, social and cultural

Inspectors are required to judge how successful schools are in promoting children's spiritual, moral, social and cultural development. The four items are, of course, of significantly different proportions although they tend to be treated as a mantra. Thinking people realize that children's spiritual, moral, social and cultural development begins at birth and, so far as we can judge, ends with death. From birth the home provides the example of beliefs, behaviour, attitudes and dialogue which shape the child's development. Between 3 and 5 years the child will be somewhere along the path of developing self-awareness, self-control, self-confidence and self-esteem. Under 60 months old the ability to reflect and communicate is affected by a mixture of maturity, experience and intellect. Young children do ponder big questions. What happens when you die? What does God look like? Why are some people disabled? Why does money come out of a hole in the wall for some people? Why do different people dress in particular ways? Children usually have clear-cut views on fairness, tempered by their experience of adult models of justice and tolerance. The trouble is that they do not show them to order.

The problem for inspectors is how to access 'evidence' of children's progress along the spiritual, moral, social and cultural paths of development. What are the markers or standards expected by 36, 48 or 60 months of age? How objective can an inspector be about these difficult issues in two days in a small school? What is the best way to record and publish the judgements in the best interests of the school and the children?

Judgement Recording Forms

The final hurdle for inspectors at this point in the inspection process are the Judgement Recording Forms. These forms are a number-crunching device to pigeon-hole the school. For example, the inspection team has to agree the number – on a seven-point scale – at which to pitch children's competence in reading and writing across the curriculum. Many inspectors think these statements are wrong because they are irrelevant for 3- and 4-year-olds. A bigger worry is that this highly subjective 'data' will be used to pronounce on schools generally or that the numbers will assume greater importance than the text of the reports.

Writing the report

Schools have more similarities than differences. Each is unique because it is a service based on working relationships. The OFSTED Framework requires the inspection report to be written under twenty-two headings. Each heading has a list of 'shoulds' that ought to be met. These twenty-three 'shoulds' include over 100 points – to be judged and commented on. While the headings ensure that each inspection and its report are looking at the same parts of school life they also act as a straitjacket for the writers. Because OFSTED emphasizes technical accuracy within defined limits it is not quality of writing that is ensured so much as formulaic writing. Such writing is boring and obscures accessibility to the general reader. The requirements leave little room for manoeuvre in the writing. Yet the report is the most visible outcome of the inspection and the feature that presents the school for public appraisal.

At present the inspection process does not emphasize enough the key inspection skills of synthesizing information in order to say what is important about a school. Too many judgements and too little time for reflection do not lead to the most constructive criticism.

Improving inspection

Inspection, done properly, matters. Successful inspection is a safeguard for the rights of children to education, play, recreation and understanding free from discrimination. It highlights the responsibilities of parents, teachers and support staff, LEAs, national government, teacher trainers and unions and professional associations to work together in the best interests of children. Reporting the story of schools safeguards the interests of the public who pay for, use and have opinions about the education of young children. Inspection that overloads schools and inspectors, which is unmanageable and feared, is unsuccessful and does none of this. OFSTED has been listening to the views of those inspected and inspecting. OFSTED recognizes that successful inspection depends on the quality of the relationship between both these partners in the process.

A revised Framework for Inspection is promised for use from April 1996. We are promised that it will pay attention to the particular place of educating younger children. It is intended that the revised process will be more manageable for inspectors and more acceptable to schools. If it does not do this why should either party continue to prop up a flawed system?

Think of the children

We are at a critical point in the history of inspection. What gradual development has counselled, self-interest now compels. All those with an interest in and a duty towards inspection must work together to make it a constructive process: a process that complements school development; a process that protects and promotes the right of young children to full development in an appropriate way.

When the complete cycle of inspection ends, perhaps in 1998, the data about schools in England and Wales will be available for analysis. This unrivalled evidence base about the health of the education system could be a new Domesday collection of facts and judgements. Then the world can judge how far England respects early years education as valid in its own right. The turn of the century will be a good point at which to ask how many good schools there are, what they are like and how we can best use them as models. We can then ask: has inspection improved children's chances of developing their personality, talents and mental and physical abilities to their fullest potential? Has inspection really worked in the best interests of the children?

Note

1. OFSTED logo.

3

Language, Culture and Difference: Challenging Inequality and Promoting Respect

Iram Siraj-Blatchford

Introduction

The title of this chapter emphasizes the need for promoting respect for all groups and individuals regardless of 'difference'. It also implies the need to challenge the oppression of individuals and groups that currently exists. Despite the calm and friendly appearance that most early child care and education settings display there may be a great deal of inequality in, for instance, the interactions, displays, policies or curriculum that staff offer. These are important issues to be considered because they concern the early socialization of both the oppressed and the oppressors. In other words, here we have a real concern for people with, and without, power to affect one another's behaviour, their actions, intentions and beliefs.

Article 2(1) of the UN Convention on the Rights of the Child (1989) states:

1. The States Parties to the present Convention shall respect and ensure the rights set forth in the Convention to each child within their jurisdiction without discrimination of any kind, irrespective of the child's or his or her parent's or legal guardian's race, colour, sex, language, religion, political or other opinion, national, ethnic or social origin, property, disability, birth or other status.
2. States Parties shall take all appropriate measures to ensure that the child is protected against all forms of discrimination or punishment on the basis of the status, activities, expressed opinions, or beliefs of the child's parents, legal guardians or family members.

In this chapter I intend to explore the ways in which children can be discriminated against on the grounds of differences in ethnic background, gender or class in either intentional or unintentional ways. Other 'differences' are significant to young children but I am here concerned with the structural inequalities which create an over-representation of members of certain groups in disadvantaged conditions. However, I do caution against the assumption that all members of structurally oppressed groups, e.g. 'all girls' are necessarily oppressed by 'all boys'. Because of the interplay between class, gender, ethnicity and (dis)ability, identity is multifaceted. I therefore argue that children may hold 'individual' positions that are contradictory to the structural position that their 'group' holds in society. Often, the interactional contexts are also highly significant.

I end the chapter by identifying the salient features of effective and ineffective practice in challenging oppression and in promoting respect for children, for parents and for staff in early child-care and education settings. The six 'levels' I identify are not meant to be prescriptive or definitive, but they are intended to stimulate discussion and thought among early years staff. A number of authors have written about the origins of inequality and about the implications for practice, and the need for a truly inclusive pedagogy and curriculum in the early years (see Davies, 1989; Lloyd and Duveen, 1992; Siraj-Blatchford, 1992, 1994; Siraj-Blatchford and Siraj-Blatchford, 1995). I argue here that children can only learn to be tolerant, challenge unfair generalizations and learn inclusiveness and positive regard for difference if they see the adults around them do the same. Children will happily imitate adult behaviour, whether it is positive or negative, they need to learn to discuss what they know, just as we do.

Identity and self-concept

The way children feel about themselves is learned and every child should have the right to feel good about her*self*. Many writers, such as Lawrence (1988), have shown that positive self-esteem depends upon whether children feel that others accept them and see them as competent and worthwhile. Researchers have also shown the connection between academic achievement and self-esteem. Purkey (1970) correlates high self-esteem with high academic performance. Working-class and ethnic minority children's poor academic performance has been well documented (DES, 1985; Bernstein, 1992), as has girls' performance in particular subjects and behaviours (Lloyd, 1987). The link between racism, sexism, class prejudice and underachievement has been thoroughly argued. However, if those who work with young children are able to undermine children's self-esteem through negative responses and behaviour then we have to evaluate our actions very carefully.

Identity formation is a complex process that is never completed. The effects of gender, class and other formative categories overlap, in often very complicated ways, to shape the individual's identity. While this chapter will not attempt to define this complexity in detail it is important for practitioners to be aware of the nature of shifting and changing identities so that no group of children or individual is essentialized and treated as having a homogeneous experience with others of their 'type'.

Positive action to promote a positive identity and self-concept should form an integral part of our work with children and this ought to be incorporated into the day-to-day curriculum. For instance, Maximé (1991) has argued that over 95 per cent of young black children in the UK are 'British black', yet they are always referred to as 'Asians' or 'Afro-Caribbeans' rather than according to their true identity. In the USA terms such as African-American and Hispanic-American have a wide currency, yet in the UK few people refer to, for example, African-British or British-Pakistani. Maximé argues that racial identity provides a necessary solid foundation upon which further learning is built. She states (1991, p. 4): 'Whether we are a builder or not we observe that the first area of focus is in constructing a foundation. A solid foundation is comparable to one's identity, that inner core which like a foundation to a building must be properly constructed and nurtured from inception.'

Geneva Gay (1985) has similarly argued that children's ethnic identity affects their whole development and learning, and that it should be seen as a vital part of each child's development. Children's feelings are an important part of their learning about themselves and others and we can make similar arguments for gender and class identity.

Some research suggests that children's attitudes and self-identity can be affected by societal stereotyping of racial groups. Cross (1985) argues that there are two distinguishable effects of racism on ethnic minority children's identity. The first is personal identity, which includes self-esteem, confidence and self-evaluation, and the second is reference group orientation, which develops racial identity, race esteem and racial ideology. Cross analyses a number of studies on ethnic minority children's self-identity and shows that most of the studies are actually about reference group orientation and not personal identity. Cross also suggests that in the USA the ethnic minority child's self-identity is on a par with that of ethnic majority children but that their reference group orientation is low and this has a damaging effect on ability of ethnic minority children to counter the impact of racism on their life experiences. A wide range of curriculum resources specifically developed to support reference group orientation is now available in Britain (Runnymede Trust, 1993; Siraj-Blatchford, 1994). A number of publications related to personal and social education (PSE) provide very useful strategies for supporting the positive development of children's personal identities (e.g. 'Circle Time'; Lang, 1995), yet few writers relate this work specifically to ethnicity.

There is now a great deal of research evidence of racial inequality at a structural level in education (DES, 1985). At the level of racial identity, culture and agency there is only an emerging literature, and most of this has been about adolescent schoolchildren (Gillborn, 1980; Mac an Ghaill, 1992). This omission is particularly interesting because issues of gender and class identities have received more attention over the years (Willis, 1977; Mahony, 1985). It is in the field of cultural studies that most writing on racial identity has occurred and this has been mainly in the areas of media studies and literary criticism. Only very recently has the focus turned to education, but again this has been focused largely on older children or students in higher education.

There has, nevertheless, been some passing recognition in British education of identity as an important concept for bilingual and ethnic minority children. The link has been made between language, culture and identity. For instance, the Swann Report (DES, 1985, p. 3) stated that 'membership of a particular ethnic group is one of the most important aspects of an individual's identity – in how he or she perceives him or herself and in how he or she is perceived by others'. But this statement is not elaborated further, or analysed, in the whole body of the report. There is no recognition of the fact that the 'whole' child may be classed, gendered or racialized in more than one way. Yet Stuart Hall (1992), for example, discusses not only the discourses of identity but also those of 'difference' within ethnic groups. In the very act of identifying ourselves as one thing, we are simultaneously distancing ourselves from something else. In terms of 'race' and ethnicity, Hall argues that there are contradictions within these categories as well as between these and other categories such as sexuality, class, (dis)ability. The way we perceive identities is very much shaped by how they are produced and taken up through the practices of *representation* (Grossberg, 1994).

Making use of the metaphor of a kaleidoscope in understanding identity based on a range of inequalities, Bailey and Hall (1992) argue that there will be differences within any identity-forming category, such as 'race'. As they put it (p. 21): 'black signifies a range of experiences, the act of representation becomes not just about decentering the subject but actually exploring the kaleidoscopic conditions of blackness'. Grossberg (1994) argues that this notion of the 'kaleidoscopic conditions of blackness' (and presumably of gender or class) is related to a 'distributive map of the social terrain' where difference is (re)created depending on how and where one is situated.

It is important to highlight the complexity of identity formation in children. To ignore it is to ignore the child's individuality. It illustrates why each black and ethnic minority child and every girl or disabled child does not perceive herself or himself in the same way. In fact, children from different structurally disadvantaged groups often hold contradictory positions, which is why we might find in our classrooms black and other ethnic minority children who are very confident and academically successful in spite of the structural, cultural and interpersonal racism in society. Similarly, we will find working-class boys who are caring and unaggressive and African-Caribbean boys who are capable and well behaved. We should not be surprised at any of this. The sexism, racism and other inequalities in our society can explain why at a structural level certain 'groups' of people have less power while others have more. But at the level of interpersonal agency we should beware of the stereotypes and focus on individual people. This is not to suggest that we should ignore structure; far from it, we need to engage in developing the awareness of children and staff through policies and practices which explain and counter group inequalities. I turn to the point of practice later. What I am suggesting is that educators need to work from a number of standpoints fully to empower the children in their care. Children need to be educated to deal confidently and fairly with one another and with others in an unjust society (Siraj-Blatchford, 1992, 1994).

In the past some researchers have dismissed non-academic identity work carried out with children as a waste of time. This critical writing has been aimed predominantly at those who teach older children. Maureen Stone's (1981) book is typical of this writing. She asserted that a multicultural curriculum distracted from the real reasons for ethnic minority children's underachievement, that is, insufficient access to, and to the teaching of, academic subjects. She suggested that a 'black studies' approach to teaching had been adopted in many schools as one way of controlling disaffected children rather than for teaching them. Much of this may have been true but none of these arguments applies to the under-8s, where it is widely assumed and recognized that a more integrated, holistic and developmental approach is needed to learning, teaching and care. In fact the case for holistic education is now being made for all children as the National Curriculum has come to dominate school time (see Siraj-Blatchford and Siraj-Blatchford, 1995).

Recent research has focused on the under-7s. Many educators have begun to ask how it is that young children who are in our care learn about and experience class bias, sexism and racism. We know that children absorb biased knowledge and understanding from their environment. This can be from parental views, media images, and children's own perceptions of the way people in their 'image' are seen and treated. In the absence of strong and positive role models children may be left with a rather negative perception of people like themselves. This bias can start from birth.

Barbara Lloyd (1987) conducted a number of studies in the late 1970s and the 1980s which illustrated how sex-biased behaviour by mothers towards babies and infants contributed toward the gender stereotyping of boys and girls. One of her most interesting studies was conducted with Caroline Smith. Both researchers observed mothers of firstborn 6-month-olds while they played with babies who were systematically presented to the mothers as either a boy or girl. The mothers responded, using their preconceived ideas of how boys and girls should behave. The same baby, when presented as a boy, was encouraged to play with a hammer and engage in vigorous activity. Conversely, when the baby was presented as a girl it was offered a soft doll and praised for being pretty and clever. Mothers appeared to favour gross-motor movements for boys.

By the age of 13 months boy infants engaged in more large motor movements while girls made more fine motor responses. As Lloyd (1987, p. 148) puts it:

> The gender differences at thirteen months may reflect babies' experiences at six months which are shaped by mothers' social representations of gender. I interpret the thirteen month olds' gender differentiated toy choice and play styles as evidence that these children are beginning to construct a concept of gender, albeit in practical activity and with some help from their mothers.

Many parents and educators conclude from childrens' behaviour that they are 'naturally' different, without considering their own contribution to the children's socialization. Difference, therefore, can be a matter of social learning as well as of physiology. This has implications for practice and the kinds of activities that we should make sure all children have access to, regardless of their gender preference.

Early years educators are often inexperienced and lack the knowledge and understanding of how children become biased and how to deal with these matters. They often display a profound sense of inadequacy when faced with sexism and racism from children (Walkerdine, 1987). Yet it is natural for children to learn the behaviours that they have been exposed to by parents and other significant adults.

Cecile Wright's (1992) research looked at the experience of South Asian and African-Caribbean children in nursery and primary schools. She selected four schools, three taking 3–8-year-olds and one middle school. Wright observed a total of 970 children and 57 staff and conducted interviews with a selection of staff and children. She offers a detailed analysis of her study. Her findings are disturbing because she has produced clear evidence that it is not only children who behave in a racist manner but also some of their teachers. She showed that both African-Caribbean and South Asian children experience racism. In particular she found that educators criticized African-Caribbean children (especially the boys) more than they did other children.

Educators also held negative stereotypes of South Asian children as lacking in cognitive ability and having poor linguistic and social skills. In terms of relations with other children Wright (1992, p. 40) found that 'Racist name-calling and attacks from white peers were a regular, almost daily, experience for Asian children. Educators were aware of the racial harassment experienced by Asian pupils, but were reluctant to formally address this issue.' It is hardly surprising that she concludes that it is generally accepted that the foundations of emotional, intellectual and social development are laid in the early years of care and education. The kind of education a child receives at this stage is therefore vital to her or his identity and future well-being.

Language and holistic education

It is through the language or languages that children speak that they actually form their sense of identity, community and belonging. The way the languages that they speak are perceived also influences the way they feel about ourselves. Unfortunately, it is still common to find individuals working within early childhood settings who view ethnic minority languages with prejudice. Such individuals typically want the children to lose their links with their mother tongue and to assimilate with the English-speaking group. Just as there is a hierarchy of valuing some 'racial' groups more than others, there is a similar racism towards languages. Recent research by Rudolph Schaffer and his team (Ogilvy, Cheyne and Shaffer, 1991) in Scotland has shown how children in multi-ethnic Scottish nurseries were treated differently, according to their ethnicity, by the nursery staff. The research reported that all the nursery staff felt they treated the children according to their individual needs. However, when the observations and videotapes of interactions between staff and children were analysed the findings were disturbing. Although the staff felt they were giving equal and caring attention to all the children, they were in reality favouring the indigenous Scottish group.

The South Asian children were reported to be receiving less attention and fewer verbal interactions, and staff used poor models of English when they explained things to them. In fact, staff often failed to attempt sustained conversations with the minority group and spoke for the children when answers were required. They resorted to a 'pidgin' English, providing a distorted version of English to the very children who most needed correct models. Research by Biggs and Edwards (1992) has provided yet another depressing reminder that children in some infant schools continue to be grossly disadvantaged by their educators. They describe their investigation of the interactions of five different teachers in multi-ethnic infant classes. As they report (1992, p. 163):

> Teachers were found to interact less frequently with Black children than White; they have fewer exchanges lasting more than thirty seconds with Black children; they also spent less time with them discussing the particular task which had been set . . . It is suggested that there is an urgent need for teachers and teacher educators to look more critically at the ways in which stereotypes are mediated through language.

Young children need to have their languages valued and their home experiences affirmed in order to feel secure enough to venture into the language and culture of their early years setting. The staff need training, knowledge and guidance on the development of appropriate bilingual programmes. Over 70 per cent of the world's population has more than one language yet in British education and care settings being bilingual is still too often perceived as an aberration, or worse, as something children should grow out of. Too often bilingual children are perceived as being merely non-English-speakers; they are perceived as a problem. Research directly contradicts this view, showing that supporting a child's home language aids the development of English learning and conceptual growth (Cummins, 1984; Verhallen, Appel and Schoonen, 1989; Pinsent, 1992) – in other words, a strong foundation in the child's home language is a necessary prerequisite to the learning of a second or third language. Evidence from a project in Bradford (Fitzpatrick, 1987) showed, for example, that Panjabi- and English-speaking bilinguals performed better in English and other areas of the curriculum when they were given the opportunity to use their home language and to be taught using their home language simultaneously with English. Ethnic minority children should be given the opportunity to acquire English as a second (or third or fourth) language in the most efficient and effective way, without prejudice to their home languages.

Identifying good and bad practice

In line with the current fashion for checklists and quality assurance criteria, I identify six 'levels' of equal opportunities practice, level zero being the least desirable and least developed practice in the area. These are based on my own and other colleagues' experiences within, and observations of, a very wide range of early years settings. Different kinds of beliefs and practices are identified which promote or hinder the implementation of equal opportunities and which allow children, parents and staff to feel valued or devalued according to the diversity they represent and the diversity in society.

Level 0: Discriminatory practice

Diversity according to gender, class, ability or cultural and racial background is seen as a disadvantage and a problem and no effort has been made to explore positive strategies for change. A separatist, or overtly racist, sexist and/or classist environment exists.

We may observe some of the following:

- Staff believe that all children are the same and that sameness of treatment is sufficient regardless of a child's gender, social class, special needs or ethnicity.
- Staff believe that no extra resources are required to meet needs based on difference.
- Parents are blamed for children not 'fitting in' to the way the setting functions and staff feel that if parents are dissatisfied with the service they should take their child elsewhere.

- Inflexible curriculum and assessment procedures do not reflect a recognition of the need for positive ethnic minority or gender role models, multilingualism in society; or sufficient observations which detect special needs.
- Staff have little or no understanding of issues of inequality, e.g. poverty, gender, racial or disability stereotyping.
- No policy statement of intent or policy documents exist relating to equal opportunities. British culture, child-rearing patterns, etc. are universalized.

Level 1: Inadequate practice

Children's special needs are recognized according to disability but generally a deficit model exists. If children who perform poorly also happen to be from an ethnic minority group this is seen as contributory. Gendered reasons may be given for poor achievement. Alternatively, the parents are blamed for being inadequate at parenting.

We may observe some of the following:

- There is a general acceptance that staff are doing their best without actually undertaking staff development for equality issues except for special needs.
- It is recognized that extra resources should be provided for English as a second language but it is felt that this is a special need which should be met by an E2L teacher or assistant, and that 'these' children will find it difficult to learn until they have acquired a basic grasp of English.
- Staff encourage children to play with a range of resources but no special effort is made to encourage girls to construct or boys to play in the home corner.
- Staff do not know how to, or do not want to, challenge discriminatory remarks because they feel the children pick these up from home, and they do not feel they can raise these issues with parents.

Level 2: Well-meaning but poorly informed practice

Staff are keen to meet individual children's needs and are receptive to valuing diversity.

We may observe some of the following:

- Token measures at valuing diversity can be observed, e.g. multilingual posters, black dolls and puzzles and books with positive black and gender role models may be found but are rarely the focus of attention.
- There is an equal opportunities policy statement but this does not permeate other documents related to parent guides, curriculum or assessment.
- Staff respond positively to all parents and children and appreciate

diversity as 'richness' but are not well informed about their culture or about anti-racist, sexist, classist, etc. practice.
- Staff development consists of occasional individual attendance at equal opportunities and special needs conferences and workshops but these are not disseminated to all staff.
- Children's home languages are valued and attempts are made to encourage parents to support bilingualism at home.

Level 3: Practice that values diversity

Generally some attempts are made to provide an anti-discriminatory curriculum and environment.
  We may observe some of the following:

- There is a centre policy on equal opportunities which includes promoting gender, 'race' and other equality issues.
- Parents are respected and staff assume that ethnic minority parents have a lot to offer.
- Staff are inhibited through worries about parents raising objections to anti-racist or anti-sexist practice.
- Staff are aware of inequality issues related to their profession and the under-representation of male and black educators.
- Resources are applied which promote anti-discriminatory work and special activities to promote racial harmony and gender and 'race' equality are practised. All children are observed carefully to detect any special learning needs.

Level 4: Practice that values diversity and challenges discrimination

'Equal opportunities' is firmly on the agenda.
  We may observe some of the following:

- The centre staff have made a conscious effort to learn about inequality through staff development and someone is allocated with responsibility for promoting good practice in the area.
- There is a policy statement on equal opportunities and a document which applies the statement of intent to everyday practice, curriculum evaluation and assessment and to the positive encouragement of anti-discriminatory activities.
- Staff observe the children's learning and interactions with equality in mind and develop short- and long-term plans to promote self-image, self-esteem, language and cultural awareness.
- Festivals are celebrated and the centre ethos uses a range of multi-cultural, multi-faith and multilingual resources.
- Staff are keen to challenge stereotypes and sufficiently confident to raise issues with parents and support them through their learning if they hold negative stereotypes.

- Staff do not tolerate racial, gender or disability harassment and have agreed procedures for dealing with any such incidents.
- Staff value the community they work in and encourage parents to be involved in decision-making.

Level 5: Challenging inequality and promoting respect

Staff actively try to change the structures and power relations which inhibit equal opportunities.

We may observe some of the following:

- The centre staff have made a conscious effort to learn about inequality through staff development and someone is allocated with responsibility for promoting good practice in the area.
- Staff value the community they work in and encourage parents to be involved in decision-making. Bi/multilingualism is actively supported.
- The management take full responsibility for promoting equal opportunities and try positively to promote their service to all sections of the community.
- Management actively seek to recruit more male and ethnic minority staff.
- The equal opportunities policy is monitored and evaluated regularly and staff are confident in their anti-discriminatory practice.
- Equality issues are reflected across curriculum, resources, assessment and record-keeping and the general ethos of the centre.
- Staff are non-judgemental and do not universalize Britishness as best, they value a range of family forms, cultures and child-rearing practices.
- Parents and children are supported against discrimination in the local community.
- Staff know how to use the Sex Discrimination Act, the Race Relations Act, the Warnock Report (DES, 1978), Code of Practice (DES, 1994), the Children Act and the UN Convention on the Rights of the Child to achieve equality assurance.

4

Choices in Learning

Wendy Scott

Introduction

The focus of this chapter is on how early years professionals can promote the United Nations Convention on the Rights of the Child through the curriculum they plan and provide in their work settings. Important factors that contribute to a high quality curriculum, such as equal opportunities, special educational needs, the value of play, assessment and record-keeping, and links with parents, are discussed in other chapters.

Teachers and other workers need knowledge about children's capabilities, and respect for both their powers and their rights to growing autonomy: children are able to make choices, develop responsible attitudes and become independent learners from a very young age provided that adults ensure that an appropriate curriculum is negotiated within a well-planned environment.

The curriculum involves the intended learning experiences on offer to the children. For under-5s, it is essential that adults plan to respond to spontaneous events as well as to anticipated possibilities in a flexible way. They need to be aware of the underlying purposes children may be exploring as they refine their skills and concepts alongside the acquisition of knowledge. It is significant that the approach to curriculum endorsed by educational theory and research reinforces the principles embodied in the Convention.

Article 42 makes it clear that the state has an obligation to make the principles and provisions of the Convention on the Rights of the Child widely known by appropriate and active means. The government's own Select Committee on Education, in its initial report on the education of children under 5 published in 1989 (DES, 1989), and its restatement published in 1994 (HC Select Committee, 1994), has taken a firm stance that is consistent with our responsibilities as signatories of the Convention.

The Report, *Starting with Quality*, of the Committee of Inquiry into the Quality of the Educational Experience Offered to 3- and 4-year-olds (the Rumbold Report: DES, 1990) laid down a strong foundation in 1990 that is entirely compatible with the articles of the Convention. This detailed advice, confirmed by cumulative research findings and further authoritative reports (National Commission on Education, 1993; Ball, 1994) provides a clear agenda for progress which must be implemented through adults' knowledge of children's capabilities and profound respect for their powers.

Theory, research, curriculum and the UN Convention

The most relevant articles of the Convention for this perspective on children's entitlement concern each child's right to express an opinion and to have that opinion taken into account, and the linked right to freedom of expression (articles 12 and 13). Article 28 highlights the importance of ensuring that discipline is administered in a manner consistent with the child's human dignity, and emphasizes the need to encourage international co-operation in facilitating access to modern teaching methods. Article 29 deals explicitly with the recognition that education should be directed at 'the development of the child's personality, talents and mental and physical abilities to their fullest potential' and 'the preparation of the child for responsible life in a free society'. These phrases are echoed in the Education Reform Act 1988, which states that 'the curriculum must . . . promote the spiritual, moral, cultural, mental, physical development of pupils at the school and of society, and prepare pupils for the opportunities, responsibilities and experiences of adult life'.

Although the statutory National Curriculum does not apply to children under 5, the Early Years Curriculum Group (1989) pointed out many ways in which under-5s were already meeting expectations of children up to the age of 7, in Key Stage 1, and encouraged practitioners to continue to work in a way that put children rather than content at the centre of their planning and recording. The group is currently working to show how the requirements of the revised programmes of study can be underpinned through a developmentally appropriate approach in the early years.

Children at the centre of their learning

A learner-centred way of working provides an effective starting point for many students, especially when they are in an unfamiliar setting and are not known to the teacher. This is particularly true for young children, whose rate of development is very individual, and whose home surroundings give them very varied prior experience. In order for them to be able to show what they can do and to flourish as learners, under-5s need to feel secure in any new context, and should have the support of adults who are able to pay sympathetic attention to their personal circumstances. This is why staffing ratios and relevant qualifications are so important. David, Curtis and Siraj-Blatchford (1993) draw attention to the key characteristics of the relationship between teaching and learning in the early years in their *Effective Teaching in the Early Years*.

Adults asking questions

Margaret Donaldson (1978) explains how young children can demonstrate sophisticated levels of comprehension when they have an understanding of the context of complex questions. She underlines the idea that adults should 'decentre' and ensure that they consider children's points of view in framing learning experiences. Often children themselves give clear indications of the lack of logic of some of our assumptions and strategies: Sonnyboy, a traveller child of 5 who had not yet learned that one of the first rules of being a pupil is to be quiet and listen, inquired of his teacher: 'Why do you keep asking the kids questions when you knows all the answers? Like . . . like . . . what colour is it then? You can see for yourself it's red . . . so why do you keep asking them?' (Cousins, 1990, p. 30).

As Katz points out (Katz and Chard, 1989), one effect of the excessive use of interrogations is to create phoney patterns of interaction, which may make respondents feel threatened. There is now a wealth of convincing evidence about the educational value of authentic discussions, where children and adults share a genuine interest, rather than sterile questioning to check whether children can provide answers that adults already know (Tizard and Hughes, 1984; Wells, 1987; Wood, 1988).

Developing language

The acquisition of language is a good example of the intellectual power of young children. It also highlights the fact that that most adults are instinctively able to provide appropriate support for children's linguistic development, and to extend their experience and skills in a way that is closely matched to progress. This is a useful model for later teaching: in addition to research on early reading and writing, influenced by Vygotsky's (1962) work on language development, there has been recent discussion on the value of a similar 'apprenticeship' approach to other forms of representation, with the adults providing a structure to match children's emerging skills (Gura, 1992; Matthews, 1995).

Culture and expectations

Cultural differences may be misunderstood by adults who are not aware of what they themselves do not know: for example, the common view that

4-year-olds should be able to use a knife and fork competently ignores the previous experience of many children who may have learned the skilful use of chopsticks or of their fingers rather than cutlery for eating at home. Although staff may not be able to familiarize themselves with every detail of children's personal frames of reference, it is certainly possible for them to share their appreciation of the varied patterns of behaviour that exist even within an indigenous group. Given a sympathetic lead, children are very quick to pick up on the ethos modelled by adults, and are well able to accept and begin to understand different expectations. Several of Vivien Gussin Paley's books vividly describe this process unfolding in her kindergarten class, expressed and explored through the children's ability to express their growing awareness through narrative (Paley, 1984, 1986, 1988, 1990).

Approaches to teaching and learning

What works for children?

Worries expressed by a government minister that an informal approach which takes into account children's individual interests will result in 'lots of fun and painting' but little serious learning are set to rest by findings from a recent project that considered attainment at the end of Key Stage 1, when children are 6 or 7. In 1994 the National Foundation for Educational Research undertook a multivariate analysis which showed that early entry to primary school for summer-born children did not result in higher achievement two or three years later (Sharp, Hutchison and Whetton, 1994; Sharp, 1995). Four-year-olds who remained in a nursery setting generally achieved better than a comparable group whose choices of both content and context were arbitrarily constrained in more formal infant classes. This is even more significant when taken together with findings that show how children may be turned off school by an instructional approach that does not take into account their past experience, their particular learning styles or their individual interests (Barrett, 1986).

Further evidence of the importance of what Dweck calls mastery (as opposed to performance) goals is quoted by Sylva (1994) and is supported by findings in her research on differences between children entering reception class after playgroup or nursery school experience (Jowett and Sylva, 1986). It appears that children who are given choices and genuine opportunities to take responsibility for their actions are more likely to use adults as a resource for learning instead of relying on them for approval, and to persevere in tackling difficulties rather than give up in the face of challenge. In order to sustain the confidence to ask questions, and to learn from mistakes, children must know that their voices will be heard and their individual needs and abilities observed and respected. This is clearly expressed in articles 12 and

13 of the UN Convention on the Rights of the Child and is also consistent with the traditional approach to nursery education in the UK. This has been well expressed by HMI in their commentary on the education of under-5s (DES, 1989) and in the Rumbold Report (DES, 1990). Many locally developed documents that guide practice across services in different parts of the country also recommend a child-centred pedagogy and counsel against too formal an approach too soon (see, for example, Westminster Education Authority, 1992; Hampshire Education Authority, 1995; Newham Education Authority, 1995).

Early childhood specialists have been promoting the value of a non-directive way of working for many years. Part of the skill of the educator is to enable a harmonious flow of activity to continue, which depends on children being able to take considerable responsibility for their own needs. Adults are thus free to work with individuals or small groups on planned or spontaneous topics. The more skilfully this is done, the easier it looks to an outside observer. It does, however, require significant forethought and organization based on professional knowledge of child development and of the individual characteristics of any particular group. There is increasing evidence to show that this kind of interactive approach, recommended and put into practice by Susan Isaacs in the 1930s and the McMillan sisters before that, is effective because it allows for physical, emotional and social growth alongside intellectual development. Recent work on the importance of the social dimension of learning (Trevarthen, 1992b) and of the long-term effects of affective dispositions to learn (Katz and McLellan, 1991; Roberts, 1995) help to explain ways of working that have already proved themselves empirically.

Developing curriculum

'Quality in Diversity', a current initiative promoted by the Early Childhood Education Forum, which aims to develop guidelines for the early years curriculum, has identified the following headings to help in the professional analysis of children's learning:

- Being and Becoming.
- Belonging and Connecting.
- Participating and Contributing.
- Thinking.
- Doing.
- Being Active.

These headings underline the integrated nature of learning in the early years, and have been devised to provide a useful framework which can be interpreted by people working with young children in different settings. Each staff group will have the responsibility of providing their own structure and activities to express in practice the principles set out in the framework. This multi-professional undertaking in the UK has been influenced by recent work in New Zealand (Ministry of Education, 1993) which envisages the early childhood curriculum as a *'whariki'*, or mat, woven from the principles, aims, and goals defined in the Ministry of Education guidelines. Different programmes, philosophies, structures and environments contribute to the distinctive patterns of the varied inter-pretations of the *'Te Whariki'* framework. Four principles (empowerment, holistic development, family and community, relationships) and five aims – well-being, belonging, contribution, communication and exploration – are identified as necessary foundations of a curriculum for children whatever form of early years provision they attend. Such an approach to the curriculum is designed to promote children's rights, and fits well with the principles and articles of the UN Convention. Every educator could examine his or her view of education and the curriculum he or she plans for children in the light of *Te Whariki*, and the headings developed by the UK Quality in Diversity project,[1] to see how his or her work links to them.

What Quality in Diversity and *Te Whariki* (and others) have in common is an emphasis on the interlinked nature of young children's learning, where physical, social and emotional development affect and are in turn affected by children's intellectual growth. They also express a profound respect for children as learners. The approach to learning adopted in the internationally acclaimed preschool settings in the Reggio Emilia region of Italy makes this respect very clear:

> Children have the right to be . . . active participants in the organisation of their identities, abilities and autonomy, through relationships and interaction with their peers, with adults, ideas, things, and with the real and imaginary events of intercommunicating worlds. All this . . . also credits children, and each individual child, with inborn abilities and potential that are extraordinarily rich, powerful and creative . . . this is so much truer when children are reassured by an effective alliance between the adults in their lives, adults who . . . place more importance on the search for constructive strategies of thought and action than on the direct transmission of knowledge and skills.
>
> (Malaguzzi, 1992)

When children in one of the preschools in Reggio Emilia were invited to describe what they saw as their own rights, one girl commented: 'Children have the right to think their thoughts, because it's them that have to think about what they want to do' (Reggio Children, 1995), and a boy stated that 'Freedom is the right to know things' (ibid.).

The fact that children around 5 years of age are able to express them-selves so thoughtfully demonstrates the profound capabilities children can develop when their views and ideas are respected and when adults find appropriate ways to work with them, enabling them to reach their full potential. These examples demonstrate the value and potential of article 28 in terms of international co-operation and the dissemination of knowledge of child development, and are reinforced by work from

North America, (Bredekamp, 1987), where the positive implications of a developmental curriculum are highlighted and examples of inappropriate practice are identified.

Resourcing children's learning

Environments for learning

Bruce (1987) confirms that children need time and scope to develop their own ideas, to explore and investigate new possibilities alongside sympathetic adults, and to engage in self-regulated practice. In order to enable this to happen, planning and organization within early years settings need to be structured to cover the wide range of learning opportunities that will lead to the kind of desirable outcomes for children entering compulsory schooling outlined by the School Curriculum and Assessment Authority in January 1996 (SCAA, 1996). In addition to providing scope for language and mathematical development, staff need to enable children to find out about the world through activities that stimulate scientific and technological exploration. An awareness of their own environment, and past and present events in their own lives, is the starting point for children's learning about history and geography. If they are to meet these expectations for 5-year-olds, under-5s need plenty of scope to investigate their world, and to express themselves creatively in a wide variety of ways.

As part of planning for all these areas of experience, and ensuring that children's physical, social and emotional development flourishes alongside their intellectual growth, staff must allow for unexpected as well as planned opportunities for learning to be followed up appropriately, assessed and recorded, and shared with parents and carers. It is useful if resources, both indoors and out, can be stored so that children can select and reach them independently, and use them to meet their intended purposes. A wide range of tools and equipment is needed to support children's learning across the curriculum, and the way that they are kept can in itself stimulate learning: for example, scrap materials such as empty cereal packets and other containers can be organized according to size and shape, so that they may reinforce mathematical thinking as well as contribute to children's physical and technological development as they construct 3D representations of their ideas. It should be possible to promote the refinement and extension of these ideas by providing a place to keep ongoing work, and by encouraging children to discuss their strategies. Children can contribute constructive comments on one another's work, and in the process become more discriminating and articulate: it is very desirable that group work should include the opportunity for more experienced learners to pass on techniques and information, as well as being the recipients of instructions themselves. Younger or less experienced children are well able to follow a lead and participate in activities which they cannot yet initiate (Katz and Chard, 1989).

Intensive, responsive, individual interaction

The role of the adult goes beyond collecting, selecting, arranging and maintaining the environment and facilitating work and play in varied groups. Evaluative, reciprocal discussion with children can encourage more accurate representations; scribing children's comments and incorporating these in a display of work reinforces both the worth of what they say and the value of literacy development. It also makes a significant contribution towards what Vygotsky (Bruner, Jolly and Sylva, 1976) called second order representation, an essential tool for later more abstract learning.

Adults should, however, hold back from telling children directly how to solve their problems: it is in choosing, experimenting and finding ways of correcting any 'mistakes' that children make learning their own, both in terms of intellectual awareness and in developing the dispositions to be selective, weigh evidence and persevere in the face of difficulties. As one of the girls at the Diana Preschool in Reggio Emilia said: 'If a child doesn't know something, she has the right to make a mistake. But this is good, because when you see the problems and the mistakes you make and after that you know, then the examples help you' (Reggio Children, 1995).

A telling example of this process of reflection and improvement being undertaken in a nursery school is shown in a video made by the British Association for Early Childhood Education. Three boys are seen collaborating in the construction of an elaborate vehicle, and then testing it. They put it safely on the top of a cupboard, and plan to come back after lunch to add wheels and further improvements. As the headteacher observes (Hart, 1994):

> By starting with what they know, young children come to understand the contribution they can make to their own learning and to their school group. This provides the positive self-image that motivates the effort and persistence needed for learning . . . through long periods of uninterrupted and self-directed activity, children learn to organise, to plan and to revise their projects and to negotiate with others.

Adults working with young children are well supported by recent publications in the UK, for example:

- Fisher (1995 and in press) explains the adult's responsibility in extending children's learning. She emphasizes the importance of giving status to child-initiated learning, and addresses children's entitlement to a broad and balanced curriculum over the time they are in the nursery setting or infant class. This has implications for assessment and record-keeping (see chapter 5).
- Lally (1991) underlines the importance of observing and following up children's own interests.

- Hurst (1991) describes some telling examples of the depth of thought young children may try to express.
- Athey (1990) provides a detailed and thought-provoking insight into the development of the invariant mental structures (schemas) that underpin young children's apparently random behaviour.
- Nutbrown (1994a) gives some enlightening examples of the implications of schemas for teaching and learning that help us to gain an insight into children's powerful search for understanding, and their profound abilities to make sense of what they encounter in the light of previous experience.
- Brierley (1987) has shown how coherent experiences lead to increased neural connections in the developing brain, and thus to increased capacity for organizing thought.

Learning across experiences

It is not easy to promote continuity in a setting with limited space, especially where children attend part-time for different sessions, but it is important to promote links across time and space as much as possible. Visits to places of interest are a good stimulus to varied representations, which reinforce learning in a variety of modalities and can be returned to and reconsidered over extended periods of time. This can be further reinforced by building on children's experience and interests at home: each child needs an ongoing relationship with adults who have an insight into the details of his or her daily experience, who can share his or her growing perspectives.

Being emotionally honest

The UN Convention is particularly relevant to emotional and social aspects of learning. Adults need to develop their awareness of their own underlying motivation in order to allow children genuine choices and freedom of expression (Drummond, Rouse and Pugh, 1992). How often does a worker, with the best of intentions, strive to cheer up a child who is upset at being left for the first time? (Difficulty on parting may happen even in a situation where appropriate care has been taken to induct both child and parents into the new setting.) It is more emotionally honest to acknowledge genuine sadness or pain, and to allow children time to recognize their actual feelings; they will respond to interesting new possibilities in due course. Another example of lack of respect for children's feelings can be seen where staff require an apology as a formula where there has been some conflict. It is more effective as well as more true to the situation to suggest something along the lines of 'I think Jo would like you to say you are sorry when you are ready' rather than to insist on an immediate apology.

Adults do sometimes allow themselves to be caught up in playing emotional games. It is desirable to give children direct messages that are more comprehensible than saying, for example, 'We don't throw bricks here', when a block has in fact just been flung across the room. A more genuine relationship can be established through the clear setting of reasonable limits. Positive reinforcement of good behaviour may have long-term dangers as well as immediate benefits: praising one child's quietness may imply that others are unacceptably noisy. Furthermore, in addition to sensing the unspoken criticism of others, children singled out for praise may tend to become overly reliant on external rewards. As Sylva (1994) and Dweck's (1988) work suggests, it is more effective to ensure that children are motivated by the learning itself rather than becoming dependent on adult approval.

Respecting children means finding out what they think and feel, and responding honestly to their ideas and emotions. It means establishing appropriate boundaries, and ensuring that each child's voice can be heard. As the educators in Reggio Emilia remind us, 'children . . . have the right to be better understood and more highly respected for what they are worth' (Malaguzzi, 1992).

From early rights to later responsibilities

As signatories to the UN Convention on the Rights of the Child, the UK is committed to ensuring that services for young children conform to standards established by competent bodies (article 3). This means that proper levels of staffing and standards of accommodation should be assured in order to protect children's rights and to promote their entitlement to high quality education and care. The recommendations embodied in the UN Convention are framed from agreed principles, but are in fact closely tied to theoretical knowledge, backed by research evidence, about effective early education. Putting them into practice will result in confident, well-informed citizens, able in their turn to fulfil their responsibilities for future generations.

Note

1. The Director of the Quality in Diversity Project is Vicky Hurst of Goldsmiths College, London.

5

Wide Eyes and Open Minds –
Observing, Assessing and Respecting Children's Early Achievements

Cathy Nutbrown

This chapter will consider, in three sections, how educators might demonstrate their respect for young children through their observations and assessments. First, I will use some stories about children and their parents to discuss aspects of observation. Secondly, I focus on assessment, what it might mean and issues leading to the notion of respectful assessment. Finally, I conclude with some ideas that educators may wish to consider if they are further to respect children's achievements.

Observing children

Children seeing with wide eyes

Children have an awesome capacity to observe in fine detail and they learn from what they see. Parents and other early childhood educators who watch young children know that they have learned so much from watching those close to them and paying attention to things they see. They learn about the uses of keys, how to pour tea from a play teapot, use a knife and fork, use computers, turn on the television, choose a favourite video, operate the video or audio tape recorder, read books, get dressed, hold conversations, hypothesize about how things work or why they have become, resolve conflicts, seek help when they need it. There is so much to learn in the early years, and learning is so complex, that perhaps it would be true to say that only young children are capable of it! Such a capacity for uninterrupted, unthwartable, multidisciplinary learning deserves enormous respect from adults.

Seeing, understanding, acting

Children approach their learning with wide eyes and open minds, so their educators too need wide eyes and open minds to see clearly and to understand what they see. If educators are blinkered, having tunnel vision, they may not have the full picture – so it's not simply a case of understanding what is seen but it is first crucial to *see* what is *really happening* and not what adults sometimes suppose to be happening. Children and the things they do need to be seen in the whole context and adults working with them must be open to seeing what *exists* not what their professional mind tells them they *should* see. Educators need wide eyes too, to guard against stereotypes and to combat prejudices about capabilities of children based on such factors as their gender, race, language, culture or disability (see chapters 3 and 6). Watching children thinking is one of the greatest privileges of any educator, and there is wide agreement that close observation is an essential process of working with young children (PPA, 1991; Drummond, Rouse and Pugh, 1992; Pugh, 1992; Drummond, 1993; Nutbrown, 1994a).

Educators need to watch the children they work with, keeping open minds and responding with sensitivity, and respect to what they see. Children need well-educated educators with knowledge at their finger-tips, adults working with them who:

• see	what is happening,
• understand	what they see and
• act	on what they understand.

Just seeing, just understanding, is not enough. The next essential stage is to take children further along their own learning pathways. This is a marker of quality in any early education provision.

The notion that young children's learning is linked with developmental patterns, or schemas, has been explored by Chris Athey (1990). Educators can provide a more appropriate curriculum which matches the developmental levels and interests of children by using their knowledge of schemas and their skills as observers to develop greater awareness of patterns of learning and understand more about children's predominant interests. The following example shows how adults' knowledge of one child's schema supported her learning and development. The educators (at her group provision and her mother at home) were seeing, understanding and acting upon what they saw.

Belinda
Belinda was 3 years old and she seemed to be tuned in to spotting or seeking out opportunities to enclose or be enclosed, and objects which enclosed. At home she enjoyed emptying and filling the washing machine, and in the garden and the bath she filled numerous containers with water

to the point that they overflowed. She and her mother built up a collection of tins and boxes that she enjoyed fitting inside one another in different combinations and she often enjoyed sitting inside cardboard boxes used to carry the shopping from the supermarket, sometimes pretending that it was a car, bus, boat or rocket. Some of Belinda's favourite books contained stories of hiding or enclosing in one way or another; stories like *Boxed In* (Williams, 1991) and *Where's Spot?* (Hill, 1980). At her sessional group Belinda particularly enjoyed playing in the house and hiding the farm animals inside the little wooden farm buildings. She dressed up and liked to play in the tunnel and hidey boxes outside.

Exploring her enveloping/containing schema, Belinda encountered much learning which linked with different areas of learning and experience. She learned about being with others and being apart, co-operating when equipment needed to be shared and dealing with her emotions when she wanted to be the only person in the house and was told to allow other children to play too. Opportunities at home and in the group enabled Belinda to explore her schema and develop her knowledge. The adults around her, sensitized to her interests, provided encouragement where a lack of knowledge may have led adults to stop Belinda doing some of the things she found interesting.

All the adults who lived or worked with Belinda were able to support and extend her learning. She encountered mathematical experiences of collecting, sorting, selecting, counting, ordering, reordering, grading, categorizing, placing. She puzzled ideas of shape and size and how things fitted together. She asked questions such as 'Why does the washing have to get covered in water before it is clean?' and 'Why do we have to wrap the potatoes before they go in the oven?', 'Why won't this one [big tin] fit inside this one here [small tin]?' Her mother extended her interest and in doing so provided more linked experiences such as involving her in baking, washing, writing letters and posting them. They looked at holes and hiding places, talked about being inside a lift and packed the shopping into boxes in the supermarket. She began to learn more about space and place relationships, finding out about relative size. Belinda's mother acted on what she saw and what she understood.

Vygotsky (1978) stressed the crucial role of the adult. Believing that adults with expertise, who were well 'tuned in' to the child they were working with, could bridge the gap (the zone of proximal development) between what a child can do with help 'today' and what – with sensitive and well-timed support – she can do 'tomorrow'. Much of Belinda's learning became possible through interaction.

Children have a right to educators with good observation skills, and the ability to match learning opportunities to a child's prevailing interest. Practice must be underpinned by theories of how children learn, and all the adults involved need to work together and make sense of what they see. Children are denied this right when they spend time with adults who are poorly trained and inadequately supported (see chapter 7).

Communication between parents and educators and continuity of experience between home and group settings is all-important. Learning experiences at home can be reinforced at the group when adults working alongside children make time to observe and understand and are able to define their own role more clearly in relation to the children.

Time must be made for ongoing, co-operative and informed dialogue between parents and educators in home or group settings if children's efforts are to be noticed and understood. This makes for a partnership of the highest order and it is an all-important factor in supporting, extending and challenging children as they learn and nurturing them through the emotional struggles that go alongside that learning. Respectful observation can occur where the climate is such that educators and parents – together – watch, listen to and talk with children.

Adults seeing with wide eyes and open minds

Adults need to make detailed and sensitive observations really to 'see' what children are doing, to make sense of their actions, to recognize their achievements and to create further learning opportunities.

> Nadia (7 months) was sitting in her high chair eating a plate of pasta and peas. Using her left hand she carefully picked up each piece of pasta with her fingers and ate them until only peas were left on the plate. Then she ate the peas, one at a time, picking up each one with her fingers, looking at it closely before putting it in her mouth.

Nadia showed any interested and attentive adult that she knew what she wanted to eat first, how she wanted to eat it, which hand she preferred to use and that she could sort different things, in this case two types of food. Young children seize everyday experiences such as eating to develop and then to apply their newly acquired abilities, and adults who watch carefully then have the opportunity to understand a little more of what they know and can do. Adults who persist in teaching children of 2 and 3 to sort coloured counters, bricks or specially purchased plastic toys need first to observe the children to see if it is a skill they already possess and use in real-life situations and therefore do not need to practise in specially created situations of dubious purpose.

As well as observing children to support their learning and understand their development adults have a role to play in protecting children and a responsibility in relation to healthy development, for as Brierley (1980, p. 17) wrote: 'Progress in education and health go hand in hand, for a sick, tired and hungry child will not learn properly.'

Charlotte

Charlotte was just 4 years old . She was admitted to the nursery when she was 3 years and 10 months old, after her mother applied for a place. Initially, Charlotte attended part-time as pressure on places in the nursery class made it difficult to offer more than a part-day place to any child other than those with special educational needs or who needed priority for some other recognized reason. Both the nursery teacher and the nursery nurse felt uneasy about this little girl; they felt that her initial attitude to them as unknown adults was wary and she seemed, even as time went on, to find it difficult to trust them. At first they put this down to natural apprehension of a new situation, but observed carefully and felt that her timidness and general lack of confidence were a cause for concern. One morning Charlotte arrived later than normal and her grandmother, who brought her, explained that the child had stayed with her the night before. That day she was very distressed and spent much of the time putting the dolls to bed and then getting them out, smacking them and telling them to be quiet. The staff observed carefully and later, during a quiet moment in the home corner, she said something in an almost inaudible voice that made the teacher think there was reason to suspect that Charlotte might have suffered some form of abuse. Events moved swiftly, bringing Charlotte, her mother and the teacher into contact with social workers, police, medical personnel, the child psychologist and the child protection liaison teacher, to name but a few. Charlotte's mother, a single parent, was most distressed, she had two other children under 5 at home and always wanted what was best for all her children. Alerted to Charlotte's behaviour and comments in the nursery, she recognized other signs that something might be happening at home and suspected a young male baby-sitter of violence towards Charlotte. This led to court proceedings and eventually a conviction. A home start volunteer offered friendship and support to Charlotte's mother to help her to cope through the distressing time, and counselling and appropriate medical treatment were arranged for Charlotte.

Michael
Both parents of 4-year-old Michael worked full time. This meant a sometimes complex arrangement for his care and education each day. Michael attended school each morning. On Mondays and Tuesdays he spent afternoons until 5.00 p.m. at a private nursery, on Wednesdays and Fridays his childminder cared for him between 8.00 and 9.00 a.m. and again from 1.00 to 5.00 p.m. On Thursday afternoons his grandmother took him to a playgroup and then Michael stayed at his grandparents' house until his parents collected him at 5.00 p.m. During each week Michael encountered five different care and education settings outside his own home and at least ten different adults were involved in his days.

At school Michael's teacher noticed that he often appeared inattentive. Knowing the arrangements made for Michael helped her to understand that sometimes this busy schedule might be a reason for tiredness that could lead to his apparent distraction and she mentioned her observation to his grandmother next time she saw her. The problem continued until eventually the teacher contacted Michael's parents and they discussed the possibility of other reasons for his distant and inattentive behaviour. He was taken to his family doctor, who referred him to a paediatrician at the hospital, and was later referred to a specialist, who diagnosed a severe hearing problem and recommended surgery.

After treatment, Michael was left with a long-term hearing problem. He was admitted to full-time school earlier than would normally be the case but in his particular circumstances it was felt that fewer settings would be in his interests. The teacher for children with hearing impairments allocated some time to Michael and helped his teacher to meet his needs in the best way and ensure that Michael had equal access to the curriculum.

Parents seeing with open minds – partnership

As the story of Belinda illustrates, parents can often see things others don't see, and through working in partnership, parents and educators can see, understand and act together (see chapters 6 and 8).

Sean

Sean was 3 ½ years old. He attended a nursery class each morning, where he spent much of his time playing outdoors, on bikes, in tents, climbing, gardening and running. His nursery teacher was concerned that he did not benefit from the other things available indoors – painting, writing, drawing, construction, sharing books, jigsaws, and so on. Even when some of these opportunities were placed outside, Sean still seemed to avoid them. The nursery teacher spoke with Sean's mother, who said: 'We don't have a garden and there's nowhere for Sean to play outside – he hasn't got a bike and there's no park for climbing, or swings around here, or a space to do outside things, but we have lots of books and jigsaws, Lego, play people, we draw and make things.' Sean was balancing his own curriculum – but the adults involved needed to observe and discuss in order to understand what he was doing.

The Sheffield Early Literacy Development Project (Hannon, Weinberger and Nutbrown, 1991) worked with parents to explore how *together* parents and the project team could promote children's early literacy. After home visits and group meetings the parents *saw* more of their children's capabilities and they *understood* more of what they saw. Children's homes and members of their families can offer powerful learning encounters. It makes sense for professional educators and families to work in collaboration, sharing their knowledge, insights and questions.

Views of assessment

Drummond and Nutbrown (1992, pp. 87–97) discussed four questions in relation to observing and assessing young children:

Why assess and observe young children?
Observation and assessment are the processes by which we can both establish the progress that has already been made, and explore the future, the learning that is yet to come.

Which children should be assessed?
Every child in every form of early years provision is a learner with a right to equality of learning opportunities. Every child's educators, therefore, have the responsibility of observing, assessing, understanding, and so extending that learning.

What do we observe and assess?
Children, and everything they do: exploring, discovering, puzzling, dreaming, struggling with the world, taking their place in it, and making their mark on it.

How do we set about observing and assessing young children?
All early childhood educators already use observation as an integral part of their daily work. The implicit, covert skills of these acts of observing can be developed, and made more explicit: the fruits of observation can be stated more confidently as we learn to record, examine, reflect and act upon the knowledge we gain through observation and assessment.

The UK government requires that all children are assessed from the age of 5. Decisions have been made about 'what counts' as 'worthwhile' assessment and, in the process, what learning is worthy of assessment. Assessment must go further than this, it must incorporate some underpinning principles that guide educators in their assessment of children. The principles of assessment underpinning the work of Drummond and Nutbrown (1992, adapted from pp. 102–3) are summarized below.

- *Respect:* Assessment must be carried out with proper respect for the children themselves, for their parents, carers and educators.
- *Care and education ('educaré'):* The care and education of young children are inseparable. Quality care is educational and quality education is caring. In our assessment practice we will recognize little children learning to love one another, as well as learning to count.
- *The power of the educator:* Early years educators must first acknowledge their awesome power and, second, use it lovingly. The 'loving use of power' (Smail, 1984) in the assessment of young children is a central principle.
- *In the interests of children:* Assessment is a process that must enhance children's lives, their learning and development. Assessment must work for children.

Views of assessment depend upon decisions about what to assess, why it is assessed, who assesses and how and when to assess. Every educator needs to consider what a respectful assessment process might look like and how to assess young children's learning and development respectfully. Wolfendale's (1993) review of baseline assessment instruments is useful in this process of consideration and decision-making. The pack,

Making Assessment Work (Drummond, Rouse and Pugh, 1992), helps educators to attend to emotional dimensions of assessment as well as philosophical, pedagogical and practical issues. The introduction to the section 'About Feelings' states (ibid., p. 21):

> Helping children to have a sense of their own self worth, encouraging them to believe that they are special, capable, unique individuals, helping them to recognize and accept the importance of their feelings about themselves and other people; these are some of the most difficult and challenging tasks all early years educators undertake. And if we are to do these things effectively, we need to think carefully about children's emotional development, and about how their feelings are affected by our words and deeds – and feelings.

In making observations and assessments of children's development – cognitive, physical and affective educators make numerous decisions. If early education is, in the terms of the UN Convention, to enable every child to fulfil his or her potential, ways need to be found to identify strengths and to support developmental needs. Key questions need to be addressed: Whose knowledge is of most worth? Is it what adults know or can assessment value what children know and the sense they make of situations they encounter? Decisions about what counts as valid goals and outcomes need to be made, and along with this goes the question of who decides: educators, governments, employers, LEAs, children, parents? The UK Prime Minister's decision to include responsibility for employment within the Department for Education in July 1995 suggested a policy position that education is for training and training is for work. It also indicated that education is about training to do a job, a narrower focus than a view of 'education for life' might suggest (see chapter 9), or the broader notion of 'lifelong learning' debated by the Commission on Social Justice (1994). Such decisions can influence ideas of 'what counts' as learning and therefore what is worthy of assessment.

A language of assessment

Different educators talk in different ways using different words about their work. These discourses employ a variety of terms and assumptions. Positive discourse about young children can include their abilities and their struggles to include themselves in the worlds of home, centre, community, that adults place them in. Other discourses take place in the media, in Government, and where observers of, and participants in, early childhood issues continue their own discourses. Terminology chosen for each discourse can contribute significantly to the debate and may influence the climate in which the discourse takes place. As Michael Rosen (1994, p. 1) notes: 'We use the same word for the educational process as we do for horse racing – a course; a predetermined sequence of obstacles that will be negotiated by all participants; anyone falling will be eliminated; only the first three give returns on bets.'

Some participants in the discourse about education choose (or adopt) the language of battle and competition: 'orders', 'standards', 'levels', 'stages', 'targets', and so on. Others choose a language more fitting to 'cherishing the growth of the young', using terms like support, nurture, cherish, development, facilitation, opportunity. Language and common understanding of the terms we use are so important. Many early childhood teachers are already 'bilingual' in some professional settings where necessary, reading, recording and communicating in the imposed language of the National Curriculum and its assessment. At the same time they may work, think, worry and discuss with colleagues and parents in the language of early childhood, the language of *educaré* (Nutbrown, 1994a, 1994b). Conversations that value children's achievements and positive discourses in early childhood are impossible without words like development, exploration, facilitation, response, support, interest, investigation, and growth.

What does respectful assessment look like?

Respectful assessment takes account of a range of factors and achievements, and values the participation of the person being assessed as well as the perspectives of those carrying out the assessment. It includes self-assessment and collaborative assessment as well as assessment of one person by someone else. There are examples of respectful assessment (Wolfendale, 1990; Barrs *et al.*, 1991; Bartholomew and Bruce, 1993; Whalley, 1994) where parents, children and their educators and carers work together to record achievement and progress and where such assessments contribute to planning further opportunites for learning.

Respecting children's early achievements

If educators observe children carefully and thoughtfully with wide eyes and open minds they will be showing children the respect they deserve, both as people and as learners. A 6-month-old baby amazes her parents with the tenacity with which she explores, how she uses every single second to find out, enjoy, request, repeat, seek. She is learning, as any 6-month-old will learn – demanding opportunities, challenging (noisily) some of the situations she finds herself in, seizing every moment – thinking about each experience, concentrating on simple things: a toy, a finger, a collar of a silky dressing gown, a spoon, a piece of banana, a reflection in a mirror, a sound, an expression. Adults who respect children's early achievements make the best educators, for they know that showing respect means accepting some responsibility.

Responsibilities

The responsibilities which early child educators and carers must shoulder in order to show respect for children's early achievements are considerable

(Drummond, 1993; Nutbrown, 1994a). People who work with young children must themselves continue to learn. If they do not continue to read, discuss and to think, to keep up to date with current issues, with theory and practice, they show a disrespect for the people they work with, the children and their parents. Systems of funding and management that do not support early childhood educators in furthering their own learning perpetuate a disrespect for young children. There must be consideration of the principles of observation and assessment and serious and continuous efforts to put them into practice. In carrying out all these responsibilities, wherever children are living and learning, ways need to be found to allow children the time they need.

Allowing children time

Time is a precious and important commodity for all human beings and most of us feel that time is remorselessly short (see chapter 9). Technology developed to enable us to accomplish things more quickly seems to have the effect of requiring us to do more in a shorter time, and adults at home and at work try to fit so many tasks into their day. But children have their own pace and while, as adults, we pursue our own (and others') timescales and agendas we need to be mindful of the need young children have to take *their* time. Pausing to listen to an aeroplane in the sky, stooping to watch a ladybird on a plant, sitting on a rock to watch the waves crash over the quayside – children have their own agendas and timescales, as they find out more about their world and make their place in it: they work hard not to let adults hurry them and we need to heed their message.

Seizing the day and biding one's time

Gardeners don't plant runner beans in January to get an earlier harvest than their neighbours; if they tried, they would probably get shrivelled and stunted beans. They fertilise the ground in the early months of the year, so that when the beans are planted – at the right time – they will flourish.

(Oxfordshire County Council, 1991)

There is a sense of urgency about childhood – of hastening progress, of accelerating development. Is this born out of wanting the best for children or from some belief or value base which says the state of childhood is worth less than the state of adulthood and so we must do all we can to reach the day when childhood is over? Gabriela Mistral said:

We are guilty of many errors and many faults, but our worse crime is abandoning the children, neglecting the fountain of life. Many of the things we need can wait. The child cannot. Right now is the time his bones are being formed, his blood is being made and his senses are being developed. To him we cannot answer 'Tomorrow'. His name is 'Today'.

This sense of urgency, the need to pay attention to children when they need it, can often become confused or be misinterpreted as the need to hasten progress. This is seen in the statutory age of schooling in the UK, where children must begin school at 5, and, even more worrying, in the current trend to admit 4-year-olds into school, endorsed by the decision of the UK government in July 1995 to issue vouchers to parents of 4-year-old children that can be used for a variety of forms of 'nursery education', including early entry into primary schools. To what extent is this plan made out of respect for children? Are its roots more securely embedded in financial and political motivations? These are questions which respectful educators – parents and professionals – would do well to ponder.

There is much truth in Mistral's words – for children it is *today* here, now, this minute that matters, but what we give them today must be made of the things *they need* today. Early intervention of the right kind at the right time bears dividends, but inappropriate intervention can cause harm. There is a mischievous mistruth in the belief that doing certain things early helps children to get ready for the next stage. The best way to help a child to get ready to be 5 is to let her be 3 when she is 3 and let him be 4 when he is 4, and to hold high expectations of what children in their first 48 months of life might achieve. The quality of experiences offered to children in their formative years are most important, (see chapter 4).

The Children Act 1989 focused attention mainly on health and safety of premises and child protection, but it is equally important to nurture healthy minds, secure emotions, grounded personalities and build on children's capacity for quality thinking (see chapter 2). Providing opportunities for healthy living and learning from birth to 5 is a way of seizing the day and biding one's time simultaneously – making the most of every moment as well as having patience and respect for the pace of childhood.

Respectful educators will strive to afford every child equality of opportunity. Not just children who are easy to work with, obliging, endearing, clean, pretty, articulate, capable, but *every* child – respecting them for who they are, respecting their language, their culture, their history, their family, their abilities, their needs, their name, their ways and their very essence. This means understanding children's needs and building on their abilities (see chapters 4 and 6).

To build on children's abilities, adults with knowledge and expertise are needed

Adult knowledge is crucial to extending children's learning and essential if children's early achievements are to be recognized and respected. Gura (1992) demonstrated how being able to discuss children's brick constructions with the correct technical language – language of mathematics, architecture, art and aesthetics – was essential in building on children's abilities. The importance of assessing children's progress is acknowledged by the School Curriculum and Assessment Authority, which describes the following as a feature of good practice (1996, p. 6): 'Children's progress and future learning needs are assessed and recorded through frequent observation and are shared regularly with parents.' Adults' knowledge about children's learning must be derived from their informed observation of them and dialogue with them and their parents.

The UN Convention on the Rights of the Child and the assessment of children

As chapter 4 illustrates, with proper respect for children and childhood we can construct a curriculum for young children which, in the words of the UN Convention on the Rights of the Child, ensures that:

> Every child shall have the right to freedom of expression: this right shall include freedom to seek, receive and impart information and ideas of all kinds, regardless of frontiers, either orally, in writing or in print, in the form of art, or through any other media of the child's choice.
>
> (article 13)

We can then find effective ways of assessing children's progress within such a curriculum.

The assessment of children in their early years must also find ways to enact the rights of children to 'the development of the child's personality, talents and mental and physical abilities to their fullest potential' (article 29).

Our view of childhood, of education, and hence the ways we observe and assess their development, can be one which respects children and their early achievements if childhood is viewed as a time of growth to be valued for itself. As Hepworth said: 'Perhaps what one wants to say is formed in childhood and the rest of one's life is spent in trying to say it.'[1] Adults with expertise who respectfully watch children engaged in their process of living, learning, loving and being are in a better position to understand what it is these youngest citizens are trying to say and find ways of helping them to say it.

Note

1 From the catalogue of the Barbara Hepworth Retrospective Exhibition, at the Whitechapel Gallery, London, 1954. Reproduced in *Some Statements by Barbara Hepworth* (Alan Browness, Barbara Hepworth Museum, 1977).

6

Children with Special Educational Needs – a Collaborative and Inclusive Style of Working

Elaine Herbert and Jenny Moir

Background

This chapter describes the collaboration between two teachers from Solihull working with children, families, school and LEA to support the United Nations Convention on the Rights of the Child, specifically that 'Children have the right to life and the best possible chance to develop fully' (article 6) and 'Disabled children must be helped to be as independent as possible and be able to take a full and active part in everyday life' (article 23).

Elaine Herbert works with an early intervention service (Pre-School Team) as a preschool support teacher working with families and their preschool children with special educational needs within the home setting, and Jenny Moir is a nursery teacher in a mainstream infant school where the nursery admits sixty children on a part-time basis (Uplands Infant School). It is inherent in what follows that in their working partnership they have developed a relationship of trust, built on mutual professional respect and a shared philosophy. As a consequence they have been able, over time, to share sensitive and confidential information without fear that it will be used in any way which is not totally respectful of the families from which it comes.

It is their contention that it is the right of *all* children to be given the opportunity to grow, to play, to socialize and to learn alongside their friends within their local community. This can take place only where the philosophy and ethos permeate from the senior management and the elected members within an LEA to its headteachers in order that the practitioners at the point of contact with the children are supported by the surrounding network. There is also a need for the community itself to have the desire to include and support children with special needs. It is the role of the professional teacher, health-care worker and social worker so to disseminate information and conviction that the community is empowered to offer this support.

The following description of the work undertaken in one small infant and nursery school shows how a community has endeavoured to accomplish these challenging objectives and illustrates what is possible.

Supporting the pre-nursery years

Early intervention is a relatively recent development (Buckley, 1994) and the Pre-School Service was set up in Solihull in 1983 as a direct consequence of the 1981 Education Act and subscribes to the Warnock philosophy of 'parents as first educators', viewing partnership with parents as 'an equal one'. Working within home settings (Herbert, 1994), there needs to be a relationship between professional and parent which recognizes the centrality of the family and the 'equivalent expertise' (Wolfendale, 1989) of both parties.

Children with a wide variety of developmental delays are referred to the Pre-School Service by professional or voluntary agencies which have first sought parental permission to do so. Visits to the home are made by a member of the team of teachers on a weekly or fortnightly basis in order to plan activities in conjunction with members of the family with the aims of enhancing the skills of both parent and child and of making an assessment over time of the child's educational needs. These activities take account of the individual dynamics of each family (Ferguson and Meyer, 1991). As this working relationship develops, the sphere of reference broadens to encompass a recognition and acceptance of the families' concerns and aspirations for their children (Rouse and Griffin, 1992).

Supporting the transition from home to school

During the child's third year he or she becomes eligible for a place at one of Solihull's thirty-two nurseries offering part-time placements for 73 per cent of Solihull children. These nurseries have a staffing ratio of one adult to ten children, and at least one of the adults is a qualified nursery teacher. It is our belief that *wherever possible* all children should enter their mainstream neighbourhood nursery alongside their peer group. Where children have special needs, the family and the preschool teacher work alongside each other and discussions take place, usually over a long period of time, about the possibility of making an application for the young child to enter nursery, and parents are encouraged to visit local schools. While parents recognize the need for their child to interact with a language-rich and mobile peer group, there is also apprehension about how others will perceive and receive their children. These fears are understandable in the context of attitudes to disability which still persist in society (Herbert and Carpenter, 1994).

Society continues to perpetuate stereotypes and respond negatively to labels, so that children with well-defined medical diagnoses such as Down's syndrome or cerebral palsy are assumed to demonstrate certain personality traits and have predictable academic abilities (Bird and Buckley, 1994; SCOPE publicity, 1994/5; *Observer* supplement 6 May 1995). In fact the range of ability and range of personality traits are as many, as various and as unpredictable as for all children. Such attitudes deny children their rights to participate as equals in everyday life – a point well illustrated by a perusal of children's clothing catalogues. Some high street shops may have begun to address the issue of including images of children with a variety of skin tones, facial features and hair types in their catalogues, but at the time of writing it is difficult, perhaps impossible, to find a children's clothes catalogue which incorporates images of children in wheelchairs, with rollators or with any obvious physical or learning difficulty. The implicit message is clear and cannot but increase the anxiety and sense of being marginalized by society that families with children with special needs experience.

Consequently, there is a natural inclination for parents to be over-protective and to fear that their child may fail and be rejected by school and community. These factors combine to reinforce the family's vulnerability in recognizing that their child may be 'special' and may be permanently different from other children. At such times they may find themselves emotionally revisiting the trauma of the initial disclosure of diagnosis (Jupp, 1992; Cunningham, 1994).

At this crucial time it is the role of the preschool support teacher to enable both family and school to act positively and to take risks in the interests of the child. Both need to be reassured that the scenario is not one of success or failure but, rather, of assessing and accommodating the individual needs of the child. Acting as a mediator between home and school, the preschool support teacher can guide each of the participants to a point of mutual trust whereby the family feels able to entrust their child to the school and the school feels sufficiently supported to welcome the challenges of the child with special needs.

The story of Mansoor describes how this support was offered to one particular family and child during this period of transition.

Mansoor was referred to the Pre-School Team, aged 2, with severe developmental delay and complex difficulties which required frequent periods of hospitalization. It was felt that a short period of assessment would confirm the need for a place in a special school. As the involvement progressed, however, it became apparent that the early predictions of his educational abilities were false. Given the new opportunities introduced by the preschool teacher and built on by his parents, he demonstrated an ability to learn quickly although the severe nature of his medical needs continued.

Eventually Mansoor's developing skills and increasing independence meant that – despite considerable misgivings – his parents realized that a nursery year would be to his advantage. An application form was given to his father, who was encouraged to deliver it in person to the headteacher in order that the control of events and the responsibility for any decisions remained with the family.

Given the intervention of the preschool support teacher and the sensitive information shared with the school about the needs of both Mansoor and his family, the headteacher made time to sit and discuss the parents' concerns with them. She made it clear that she valued them as equal partners and did not belittle their anxieties.

The application was accepted and the way was prepared to introduce Mansoor to the school. This little boy had never been separated from his parents before. In the term prior to nursery, it was decided to use the time allotted by the preschool support teacher to that family to carry out a programme of gradual separation from home and introduction to school. This took several weeks and involved a collaborative approach by the parents, the preschool support teacher and the school. The family was totally involved in all the planning and was able to celebrate each small achievement. This programme was very successful and enabled Mansoor and his family to begin the nursery year with confidence. Mansoor completed his nursery year and was able to progress into the main school without any additional educational support for his learning although his medical needs continued to require intervention.

Managing support within the school community

At Uplands Infant School the headteacher commands a pivotal role in determining appropriate attitudes and levels of commitment by staff in her school, to ensure that the rights of children are upheld (Bastiani, 1989). There is an expectation that all children whatever their needs will be given an equal degree of care and respect from class teachers, classroom assistants, dinner supervisors, voluntary helpers and visiting professionals (Siraj-Blatchford, 1994).

There is an acknowledgement that the special educational needs of children come within the remit of every class teacher and that it is the duty of teachers to attend not only to what is 'special' but also to what is 'ordinary' in every child (Dessent, 1987). The very small steps accomplished by the child with special needs are celebrated alongside the achievement of the most able pupil (Wolfendale and Wooster, 1992).

It is part of the ethos of the school that equality of opportunity does not mean offering the same to all children. There are occasions when rules and routines have to be adapted to enable particular children to participate more effectively in the life of the school.

Jane, who has cerebral palsy, made her way around nursery on a rollator. In order to keep up with the other children as they moved from one routine to another, she was encouraged to predict her needs within the structure of the nursery day so that she became responsible for being in the 'right place at the right time'. This often involved her moving ahead of the other children, for the alternative would have been to resort to carrying her around the nursery. However, on days when new splints were painful or a bout of ill-health left energy levels low, Jane could ask to be carried – *but the choice and the control were hers.*

The school also acknowledges that the community as a whole is enriched by the inclusion of children with special educational needs. Opportunities to develop friendships with children with a diversity of needs enhance the skills and understanding of all children (Lewis, 1995).

Steven, a child with Praeder Willi syndrome (a chromosomal disorder resulting in general developmental delay), joined the nursery at the request of the Pre-School Team. Prior to nursery his social contacts had been with devoted and caring adults and as a consequence he was heavily dependent on adult support and had no strategies to enable him to interact with his peers. Carl joined nursery at the same time and presented as an earnest and highly articulate little boy who did not find the boisterous play of many of his peers easy to accommodate. Within the first term of the nursery year Steven and Carl developed a friendship. Steven appeared to recognize and relate to Carl's mature, managing and articulate persona and Carl gained great self-esteem from finding himself able to act as Steven's special friend, guide and mentor.

Initially, Steven was able simply to access 'tried and tested' play areas (sand at home, sand at nursery). Carl began to invite (perhaps, order!) Steven to accompany him round the nursery. Thus both children were enabled to explore and experience all areas of the nursery curriculum to their mutual benefit (Ainscow, 1995). Although their friendship began as an exclusive one, gradually the confidence each gained through the support and companionship of the other enabled them slowly to include others in their play, and both children learnt important social skills which eventually led to the acquisition of wide friendship circles among their peers.

Similarly, when Daniel, a child with a severe speech disorder (dyspraxia) entered nursery, his peers needed to learn and understand that some children communicate using signs and that although they could talk to him as to other children, they could not expect interactive conversation but needed to look for his gestures and signs. Daniel had to manage the frustration of not always being able to make himself understood but discovered that he was an expert at signing within the context of the nursery and was able to teach his language to both adults and children.

Nursery parents delighted in their children's new understanding and skills, and visiting parents would try hard to interpret Daniel's signs. In fact, one mother so appreciated this shared experience that she asked

Daniel's mother for advice about how to learn Makaton[1] and borrowed an introductory video from Daniel's family. Thus Daniel's presence in nursery facilitated an enriching learning experience for all participants, children, parents and staff.

A school which regards it as a privilege to share in the experiences of a child with learning difficulties is a school which is at least attempting to uphold the rights of every child to 'develop fully' and 'to take a full and active part in everyday life'.

Managing support within the classroom

If children find learning difficult it could well be that there is something wrong with the way we are asking them to learn.

(Smith, 1982)

Although the familiar arguments for sufficient funding to support children with special educational needs in the mainstream classroom are not to be underestimated, all available funding is liable to be ineffectual if the attitudes and aspirations of the professional adults are not committed to and supportive of an inclusive or integrational philosophy (Clark, Dyson and Millward, 1995) The interpretative eye of the classroom teacher needs to be informed by these attitudes when she observes what is happening in her classroom (Lewis, 1991). She needs to look for success, not for failure. While being observant of deficits and sensitive to the need to adapt the curriculum accordingly for individual children, she needs also to be observant of elements of progress, measured against an individual baseline of achievement not according to general group expectations.

David, who had a profound hearing loss and cerebral palsy, arrived at nursery with little or no experience of children of his own age. However, it was the opportunity to interact with other children which appeared to give David the motivation to make eye contact with play equipment and other people and thus begin to learn a range of new skills, alongside his peers, which were valued and celebrated alongside the more sophisticated and complex learning of his peers.

Not all learning is the result of adult planning and intervention. Important incidental learning can take place in response to the opportunity to be part of this nursery community. It is the role of the teacher to recognize, value and support this learning as it emerges (Drummond, 1993).

Nicola had general learning difficulties and delayed speech and language. As for all children with special educational needs, Nicola's parents were offered the opportunity to share in a home–school liaison book, to enable Nicola's adult carers both at home and in school to talk to her about significant parts of her day. This book was used informally by her parents and nursery staff. However, it became apparent that events perceived as important by the adult often did not coincide with those selected by Nicola herself.

This happened for the first time on the day that Bruin, the teddy bear puppet, was introduced to the children at school. The nursery teacher included this event as the predicted highlight of Nicola's day. In fact, Nicola dismissed all of her mother's efforts to elicit interest in Bruin and would only point to one of her fingers and repeat 'poorly'. That day, the nursery teacher had sported a small blue plaster covering a cut on her finger. Nicola had pointed to it and had been told by the teacher that she had a 'poorly finger'. Thus, for the first time, Nicola communicated information about events in nursery without the promptings of the information given to her family in the liaison book: an exciting and highly significant step forward in her independent language skills.

This was the first of many instances of Nicola demonstrating a persistent interest and concern for the well-being of others, and was an area of interest and learning that the adults in her life were able to support and extend throughout her nursery year.

In addition to observing children's learning in these positive ways, the classroom teacher also needs to develop confidence in evaluating her practice in such a way as to believe that the skills she has in providing a well-structured and stimulating learning environment for mainstream children are equally relevant to the child with special educational needs in her care. She needs to understand that there is no mystique in supporting children who have learning difficulties (Lewis, 1991). We can all learn to analyse tasks and make them accessible to an individual child. The preschool support teachers, and other teachers specializing in accommodating the learning styles of children who need individual programmes of study, are there as a resource for the mainstream teacher. The classroom teacher needs to remember that a given label of medical diagnosis, or the brief description of a special need, should not deflect her from normal good practice of modifying and differentiating by task and outcome for *all* children (David, 1992a).

Expectation of *all* children must be realistically high. One should not feel it is 'kind' not to expect too much, when in fact every child has the capability to strive for new horizons. Equally, excuses should not be made for unacceptable behaviour. Alysha, a little girl with a confirmed diagnosis of autism, could only reasonably be expected to join in group action rhymes and songs when sitting on an adult's lap (Carpenter, 1995). Sally, a child with general learning difficulties, needed kind but firm guidance to encourage her to become an accommodating participator in the group. Both children would have preferred to roll and run around during these activities but both were encouraged and enabled to become group members in a way which was meaningful and appropriate for them. Only the highest expectations and demands made of all children can contribute to a programme of inclusion which is genuinely working to ensure that each child is being offered the opportunity to 'develop fully' and is 'helped to be as independent as possible'.

The class teacher has a responsibility to balance the needs of the individual with the needs of the group. There are a few children who because of either the severity or complexity of their difficulties require constant adult supervision on a one-to-one basis, either to gain physical access to the group or to ensure the safety of themselves or others. In extreme cases, their integration can become locational rather than genuinely inclusive and then the particular need of an individual to learn within the mainstream nursery can be outweighed by the needs of the group.

Let us consider Kate's experience. In nursery Kate threw toys, often hit and pushed her friends and required constant supervision as she loved to open doors and run out of the nursery. A highly specialized programme of intervention was needed that could not properly be embarked upon in the nursery if the needs of the other children in the group were not to be compromised. Kate left nursery after one term to move to special provision where this level of support was available. The decision had the full support and co-operation of her parents and all professionals involved. This consensus was achieved in what could have been a very difficult situation. Prior to nursery assessment, no predictive judgements had been made. Kate had been given the same opportunities as her peers and her parents had been given the opportunity to spend time in the nursery to observe their daughter and gradually accommodate the notion that such a placement did not meet her needs. In this case too, respectful educators maintained the rights of all children. During this difficult period of transition, the preschool support teacher with her flexible pattern of working was able to increase the level of support to the family as it struggled to come to terms with the newly perceived parameter of Kate's educational needs. The thoughtful caring and efficient management of such a scenario needs to be clearly articulated to governors, nursery parents and the family of the child with special educational needs, so that all concerned can feel empowered to take risks and to ensure that the best interest of each child is paramount, as identified in the Children Act 1989 (Whalley, 1992).

The additional support that so often needs to be available to the family with a child with special educational needs can be problematic for the mainstream class teacher. Families who have experienced the nurturing and supportive one-to-one relationship with the preschool support teacher, prior to attending nursery, may find it difficult to accept the more limited support available from a teacher who has twenty-nine other families to support simultaneously. Parents of children with special needs have spoken, on the one hand, of their desire not to be perceived as different by other parents or members of staff but, on the other, of their additional need for information about their child's progress in order to inform their future decision-making and satisfy themselves that things are 'right' for their child. They do not wish to appear attention-seeking as a consequence and may have high levels of anxiety about what the teacher may have to say about their child (Mittler and Mittler, 1994; Hornby, 1995).

It is the teacher's responsibility to ensure that there is a constant exchange of information between home and school so that she is able to support appropriately the child's learning in the nursery (Nutbrown, 1994a and b). Parents not only love and care about their child, they also meet the whole range of professionals involved with the child (doctors, speech therapists, physiotherapist, etc.) on a regular basis and are therefore vital links as well as partners in the interdisciplinary pattern of working. To facilitate exchange of information, the class teacher must always give a positive welcome while acknowledging that time is limited. However, the preschool support teacher can usefully intervene at this point to 'fill the gaps of communication' using the good relationships already established with both home and school. If this collaboration is founded on a philosophy of a shared purpose, acknowledgement of equal if different expertise and a sense of trust (Pugh and De'ath, 1989; Wolfendale, 1989), then the best interests of the child will be better met.

Perhaps these issues can be illustrated by the experience of working with Claire, the mother of Amy, a child with Down's syndrome. Claire arrived punctually and regularly to deliver and collect Amy each day. She had chosen Uplands Nursery having been reassured by the preschool support teacher of the welcome she and her child would receive. However, as the early weeks of the nursery year passed, it was observed that Claire avoided all eye and social contact both with other parents and with nursery staff. The nursery teacher sought the help of the preschool support teacher who was known to have a close, professional relationship with Claire. During informal precisely focused conversations at home, it emerged that Claire had heard tales of a mother who had attended a different nursery in the previous year and become distressed and demoralized by the daily descriptions of what her child could not do when compared with his peers. Claire had decided it was safer to arrive at nursery, but to ask no questions.

Through her mediatory role, the preschool support teacher was able to reassure both Claire and the nursery staff that all was going well and was able to instil confidence. Nursery staff on the advice of the preschool support teacher continued in their efforts to develop a friendly relationship until eventually a genuine sharing of information became possible. Indeed the management of Amy's learning developed to include all three members of the partnership, working on shared targets, and using consistent behaviour-management strategies to support her learning both at home and at school. This collaboration between the families of children with special needs, the preschool teacher and the nursery enables optimum use to be made of the integrated setting of the nursery. The advantages of such a setting over the more traditional segregated special unit or school seem to be that children can be observed alongside their peers and can be given the opportunity to access a curriculum considered developmentally appropriate for preschool children. Additional support, to aid social or cognitive learning opportunities, is implemented only when what is offered as standard proves inadequate. Such a setting can therefore be described as a more realistic yardstick of human behaviour (Burns, 1985).

Managing support through the formal process of assessment

The Code of Practice for the Identification and Assessment of Children with Special Educational Needs (DFE, 1994) acknowledges (para. 5:22) the 'significant changes which can take place in the progress of a child under the age of five'.

Given the ratio of one adult to ten children provided by Solihull LEA in its nurseries, opportunities are already in place to support most children with special educational needs within the mainstream for this nursery year. It has been our experience and is now our conviction that there is a need to delay the formal stages of the assessment process for these young children for as long as is possible. Predictions made either before nursery in a one-to-one involvement in the home or even during the first term, when the process of adapting to a new setting is being established, can be highly prejudicial to a true representation of a child's particular needs.

We can recall Jane who has cerebral palsy. Prior to nursery it was felt that additional adult support might be needed to respond to her physical disability. It was because of the above conviction that the preschool support teacher and nursery staff, supported by the headteacher, resisted this level of intervention at this stage, preferring first to observe Jane *in situ* and then respond to any needs which might arise. It was found that the addition of simple aids, such as a handrail in the toilet, was all that was needed to enable Jane to be independent and actively participate in nursery alongside her peers.

Inherent in this desire to delay formal assessment for as long as possible is the understanding that information gathered in the nursery setting, about group interaction and learning, cannot effectively be gathered elsewhere and time must be allowed for this process to take place. Nursery staff need time to adjust to the needs of a child with special educational needs. Parents of the child with special needs need time to be able to make relationships with nursery staff and spend time in nursery so that observations can be shared, discussed and assimilated. Parents are then in a better position to approach the formal statutory assessment as fully informed and empowered participants in the decision-making process (DES, 1994).

As the reception year approaches, the fact that the favourable adult-to-child ratio will disappear has to be taken into account as a major part of the equation when considering the needs of the child with special educational needs (David, 1993). Some children supported in nursery by the preschool teacher do enter reception classes alongside their peers and are deemed to need no extra help over that offered to other children. Instead they would constitute a part of the 18 per cent of children recognized in the Code of

Practice as having their needs met by the implementation of school-based procedures of assessment and intervention.

For others it becomes clear that there is a need to request formal statutory assessment and in many cases such an assessment has resulted in a statement of special educational needs. Since the Code demands that the process should take no more than six months and since there is an acknowledgement within the Education Act that young children have rapidly changing needs, the headteacher of Uplands School made a formal request to the special needs officers that the school be permitted to delay the presentation of reports to parents and LEA officers for as long as possible. The special needs officers responded with flexibility and have supported the school in its request – a scenario which illustrates the need for a shared philosophy permeating from senior management within the LEA to the schools which it supports.

As the assessment progresses through the formal stages all involved professionals need to be aware of the trauma involved for the parents of children with special educational needs. It is now that they must finally acknowledge that their child is, in some areas of development, different from her or his nursery peers (Carpenter and Herbert, 1994). The predictability of what we all know about going to school has evaporated into a path which leads in new and only partly comprehended directions. Information and emotional support can be offered most effectively if the collaborative style of working has been well established and open communication and a sense of trust exist between parents, preschool teacher and nursery staff (Rodd, 1994).

If we return to Amy and her mother, Claire, at this stage of the assessment procedure, we can see how this established triad of relationships helped to ease a very difficult time for this family. The recommendation of the statutory assessment was that she should attend a mainstream school with additional classroom support. While Claire understood that Uplands School would have welcomed the opportunity to work with Amy in the reception class, they were a committed Christian family who felt that all their children should attend a church school. The continuing relationship with the preschool teacher enabled the parents to discuss the pros and cons of their choice of school for Amy without fear of embarrassment or offence. In fact, the preschool teacher was able to help the family to feel able to share these feelings and concerns with nursery staff and the headteacher of Uplands School. There was no breakdown of communication and the parents were able to access all the information they felt they needed to make a decision. After much thought, heart-searching and discussion, they requested that Amy's statement name the church school, and their request was respected and acceded to by the special needs officer.

For some children their inclusion in the nursery or in a reception class can be accomplished only if additional adult support is given. When managing such a scenario it is important to remember that by choosing the inclusive option one has accepted that the child needs to interact with her or his peers and not become dependent upon a one-to-one adult/child relationship. Young children learn not only from an adult's instructions but also by following a peer group model. If the additional adult support gets in the way of this peer group interaction by an excess of withdrawal-based input or constant intervention in their play, the child is not appropriately supported. The role of supporting adult is a skilled job which requires both a higher profile and a greater degree of training than is often afforded.

Finally, one of the duties of all professionals involved in guiding a child through the procedures outlined in the Code of Practice is the necessity of presenting written reports to both parents and special needs officers. It is the policy of both the Pre-School Team and Uplands Infant School that no information should ever be transmitted to parents for the first time via a formal report. If the ongoing process of communication outlined above has been established, then the presentation of a report is only a formal summary of previous discussions (Jowett, Baginsky and MacNeil, 1991).

Written reports should be presented in such a way that the philosophy of respect for the family and child, the acknowledgement of equal if different expertise and the sensitivity to the needs arising out of 'transitional trauma' are all upheld.

Implications for practice

When working with children with special educational needs and their families, educators need to:

- respect and nurture what is unique in every child;
- develop respectful attitudes towards the children and their families, accepting that all families are different. It is the role of the professional to empower and enable the family to make its own judgements, choices and decisions and to support them in accepting responsibility for these;
- evolve a flexible pattern of working in order to respond to the changing needs of families, by supporting them both in moments of crisis and in times of consolidation;
- develop a collaborative pattern of working to ensure that all participants share a purpose and acknowledge the equal, if different, expertise of all involved – parents, teachers and representatives from other disciplines. This should be supported by a rigorous programme of personal and professional development;
- acknowledge that families of children with special needs work alongside a wide range of professionals. There is a need to accept and respect the close relationship the family may have with any one of these professionals. This chosen professional should then be consulted as a key worker for that family;

- articulate an inclusive philosophy which contends that both the needs of the child with special educational needs and her or his mainstream peers are better served when opportunities to share experiences are available;
- develop positive attitudes which do not rely on prediction or first impressions but, rather, work to assess over time, through observation, recording and evaluation;
- maintain high expectations of all children. Teachers need to respond to individual needs as they arise rather than to stereotypes suggested by medical diagnostic labels;
- ensure that, when individual adult support is allocated to a child with special educational needs, it must be so managed that it enables the child to interact with her or his peers and achieve independence of both thought and action;
- be supported by a professional network to enable the worker at the point of contact with the child to work positively and creatively, thus serving the best interests of the child and her or his family.

Conclusions

This chapter has demonstrated how a collaborative and inclusive pattern of working with families and their children with special educational needs can benefit the community as a whole and serve to uphold the right of all children to 'develop fully'.

With the growth of testing, the increase in baseline assessments and the advent of National Curriculum SATs and league tables, it should be remembered that many of the benefits of the above style of working are not measurable by such yardsticks. In this climate of accountability, a methodology to evaluate rigorously such patterns of learning must be devised to ensure its development for future generations of children.

Note

1 Further information about the Makaton Vocabulary Development Project can be obtained from MVDP, 31 Firwood Drive, Camberley, Surrey GU15 3QD.

7

Do We Train Our Early Childhood Educators to Respect Children?

Audrey Curtis

This chapter is being written at a time when professionals, parents and the general public are considering the implications of the 'voucher' scheme launched by the Secretary of State for Education and Employment. It opens up a new approach to provision for young children and with it the possibility of providing all 4-year-old children with three terms of good quality preschool education. Parents are to be given the opportunity to decide whether to use state, private or voluntary providers. In introducing the scheme the Secretary of State has stipulated that every institution wishing to take part will be required to provide education appropriate to stated learning achievements and there will be 'light touch' inspections carried out to ensure that the institutions are maintaining appropriate standards (see chapter 2).

Few would disagree that all children should be entitled to good quality early childhood education – most of our European neighbours provide high levels of quality provision for children from 2 or 3 years of age. However, good quality provision can be offered to children only if the workers are all trained at an appropriate level and the staffing ratios are adequate. There is substantial evidence from the USA to suggest that high quality provision depends more upon high quality professional practice than on any other single environmental circumstance (Saracho, 1992).

In 1995 Lord Walton, writing a year after the report of the National Commission on Education (1994), stated that 'high quality learning depends above all on the knowledge, skill, effort and example of teachers and trainers' (Walton, 1995). Later in the same paper he wrote (ibid.) 'At the heart of high quality learning is high quality teaching.'

In examining the various types of training programmes for working with young children it is essential that we consider the rights of the child and not focus our attention upon the needs of parents, workers or administrators who frequently make provision in their own best interests.

The United Nations Convention on the Rights of the Child, accepted by the UK government in 1991, has now been ratified by 144 countries. It sets out a number of articles relating to the rights of children and young people up to the age of 18 years. The children to whom I am referring in this chapter are the youngest, ranging from 0 to 8 years of age. There are eight articles in the Convention which I believe have particular relevance to the issue of training.

Article 2   All the rights in the Convention apply to all children equally whatever their race, sex, religion, language, disability, opinion or family background.

Article 3   When adults or organizations make decisions which affect children they must always think first about what would be best for the child.

Article 12   Children too have the right to say what they think about anything which affects them. What they say must be listened to carefully. When courts or other official bodies are making decisions which affect children they must listen to what the children want and feel.

Article 13   Children have the right to express what they think and feel so long as by doing so they do not break the law or affect other people's rights.

Article 23   Disabled children must be helped to be as independent as possible and to be able to take a full and active part in everyday life.

Article 28   Every child has the right to free education up to primary school level at least. Different kinds of secondary school should be available for children. For those with ability, higher education should also be provided.

Article 29   Schools should help children develop their skills and personality fully, teach them about their own and other people's rights and prepare them for adult life.

Article 31   Every child is entitled to rest and play and have the chance to join in a wide range of activities.

Training to work with young children

Teacher education

Currently there are two main routes to becoming a qualified teacher. The main route for early years teachers is to follow an integrated B.Ed. degree within which National Curriculum subjects and education form the main studies. The other route, which is becoming increasingly popular, is a one-year postgraduate certificate in education, which is very school-based (two-thirds in schools and one-third in college/university). A different route into teaching is via the licensed teacher scheme. This is mainly for recruitment in shortage subjects like modern languages and physics. It is a school-based training scheme open to anyone who has a minimum of two years' study in higher education.

During the last few years early childhood teacher trainers have expressed deep concern that the changes in teacher training courses have forced them to move away from their traditional child-centred approach to training towards one which is subject-based. The new three-year B.Ed. course with its emphasis upon subject teaching, and, for the youngest children, a narrowly defined skills curriculum of literacy and numeracy will go against all the principles of early childhood education. The concept of a broad-based, integrated approach to the curriculum has long been the hallmark of good early years practice. One of the dilemmas posed by this approach is the way in which it could sever the traditional links between nursery and infant school teachers.

Sylva, in the recent RSA report (Ball, 1994), has argued that the best solution to this dilemma would be to combine nursery and infant teaching and offer a graduate training for all who work with children from 0 to 6 or 0 to 7 years. This is the system which has been introduced in Spain.

Most of the existing B.Ed. courses do not cover work with the under 3s and only a few prepare teachers adequately for work with children from 3 to 5 years. The recently trained nursery teacher is not likely to have had more than a short theoretical course and only one practice in a nursery school or class.

Traditionally, it has always been considered that a sound knowledge of child development was fundamental to the training of early years teachers. Compared with our counterparts in Europe the early years teacher in the UK has far less training in child development. In a recent survey of twenty-four European countries I found that for early years teachers child development was a major component of training, with considerable emphasis placed upon the need to be aware of the affective domain, an area which receives little attention in our programmes (Curtis, 1994). Likewise in Australia, New Zealand and the USA child development is an essential component in every training programme. Only in the UK does it appear that we have reduced the amount of child development which we offer to students training to work in nursery and infant classes. This is a multidisciplinary study, drawing on all the disciplines relevant to our understanding of children. Quite properly these courses are no longer taught as separate disciplines but, rather, as integrated studies. Early years educators need the integrated knowledge if they are to work effectively with young children and their families.

Recently several universities have introduced B.A. degrees in Early Childhood Studies (such as those at Manchester Metropolitan and

Bristol Universities). These offer students the opportunity to study at depth a broad range of issues relating to early childhood education. A PGCE following such a degree would provide the teacher with a sound specialist knowledge of the early years.

Do teacher training programmes respect children's rights?

Certainly all our programmes train teachers to provide children with a sound knowledge-based primary education. During their school experience student teachers learn how to develop various skills and competences in children. Government regulations lay down the number of hours to be spent on courses relating to children with special educational needs and have stressed the necessity of including courses on equal opportunities, anti-discriminatory practice and child protection. Hopefully, most student teachers are aware of the main clauses in the Convention on the Rights of the Child. It would be interesting to investigate whether they were as informed as the Japanese student teachers questioned by Ishigaki (1995).

Children are encouraged to play and develop leisure activities. Although the legislation is in place to protect children's rights, in practice, parental and other pressures are substantially reducing the amount of time children have for leisure and play. Early years classes are becoming increasingly teacher directed, with play no longer an integral part of the learning process. Many children rush from nursery or infant class to ballet or music classes, riding lessons and sessions in the gym. The time for free choice and freedom to play becomes increasingly limited (see chapter 9).

As the B.Ed. programme becomes shortened and more focused on the subject knowledge needed to deliver the national curriculum (Dearing, 1994), there is a very real danger that the time allocated for understanding *how* children learn and develop will decrease and issues like child protection and anti-discriminatory practices may be dealt with in a cursory manner.

Nursery nurses

The largest group of professional early years workers are the nursery nurses who study the care and development of children from birth to 8 years. The majority of nursery nurses follow a two-year course leading to the Diploma in Nursery Nursing or the B.Tec. Diploma in Nursery Nursing. The courses are modular and cover all aspects of children's health, care and education. Social and family studies make up a large part of the course and there are modules dealing with anti-discriminatory practices, equal opportunities and child protection. These are the only non-medical early childhood nursing courses which deal with babies and children under 3 years of age. The training of nursery nurses –

whether the awarding body is the B.Tec. or the Council for Awards in Children's Care and Education (CACHE) – has a strong practical element and students are expected to spend up to half their training in the practical placement.

Although not at a high academic level these courses encourage the candidates to develop skills to provide a high level of care for children. Until recently, however, there has been relatively little emphasis in training on the educational provision for young children particularly for children in the infant schools. In this respect the needs of the children are not being met. This should be of concern to everyone as an increasing number of nursery nurses are to be found in the private sector day nurseries, a rapid growth area, as it raises questions as to how the able 3–5-year-olds are intellectually challenged.

Much of the work which is carried out in the day nurseries at this level is adult-orientated at a time when we are well aware that the most stimulating and challenging environments are child-centred and focus upon respect for and needs of the child.

The Advanced Diploma in Child Education which is offered by CACHE goes some way to fill the gaps in the initial training courses as this modular diploma provides opportunities for experienced early childhood workers to gain the necessary underpinning knowledge needed to promote children's cognitive development.

National vocational qualifications in child care and education

A third and very different approach to training to work with young children was formally launched in February 1992. Six years earlier, the government, concerned about the level of qualifications in the UK workforce, established the National Council for Vocational Qualifications, which was charged with reforming and rationalizing the whole approach to vocational qualifications across all occupational sectors.

It was intended that the new national vocational qualifications (NVQs) would be based upon nationally agreed standards of competence to do a job and would be assessed primarily in the workplace. The underlying rationale was that NVQs would break down barriers to access to qualifications through abolishing formal educational requirements and give credit for knowledge and competence acquired in non-traditional ways. In this way those already employed could achieve a national qualification without leaving their employment.

Each NVQ or SVQ (Scottish vocational qualification) comprises a number of 'units of competence' which are of value in employment. The candidate can build up these units as credits towards a full award over a period of time. There is no fixed time limit, although CACHE requires candidates to re-register after five years if they have not completed their award. There are no formal academic entry requirements and candidates can offer themselves for assessment when they are ready, regardless of how long it has taken them to become competent or the ways in which they studied to prepare themselves for assessment.

This approach is radically different from the other methods of training which have been discussed as these are based on study connected with an institution and involve following a syllabus and learning skills and knowledge within a given period. The focus of the NVQs is on achieving 'outcomes' in the workplace in terms of the functions which a competent worker should be able to carry out and the knowledge he or she uses to perform competently.

There are five levels of competence ranging from level 1, which is at the most basic level with the worker requiring constant supervision, to level 3, which involves competence in a broad range of competences and considerable responsibility and independent working. Level 4 is at the managerial level and level 5 is the equivalent of a senior professional. NVQs exist in more than 80 per cent of the occupations in the UK. Those in child care and education started later than many of the other occupational standards.

In 1989 the Care Sector Consortium, the industry lead body, commissioned the 'Working with Under Sevens' project. Its remit was to develop occupational standards of competence for those who work with young children and their families. The group, led by Denise Hevey, used functional analysis techniques to analyse the work of child carers and, with the help of more than 3,000 practitioners and managers from all over the UK, the national standards in child care and education were developed.

The practitioners came from the private, public and voluntary sectors of the community, ensuring that the standards incorporate the values and principles which are so important to early years workers and reflect their commitment to the 'care' and 'education' of young children.

In the official handbook (*National Occupational Standards for Working with Young Children and their Families*, 1994) it is stated that where possible the following principles have been integrated into the performance criteria of the standards:

- demonstrating a caring and considerate attitude towards children and parents;
- recognizing the crucial role that parents play and working in partnership with parents whenever possible;
- meeting all aspects of children's developmental needs;
- treating and valuing children as individuals;
- enabling children to be directors of their own learning;
- promoting equality of opportunity;
- celebrating cultural diversity;
- using language that is accessible and appropriate;
- sharing information and liaising with parents and other professionals;
- ensuring the health and safety of children and others;

Owing to the nature of the work and the fact that child-care workers are never in a totally supervised role it was decided that there would be no level 1 in child care and education. At present there are only levels 2 and 3, although a managerial level 4 is being planned for the future. Launched in February 1992, the standards in child care and education comprise ten units at level 2 and fifteen units at level 3. Four units are common to both levels. Besides the core elements there are a limited number of endorsements for each level which allow for a degree of specialization to meet the needs of different settings, for example 'work in support of others' and 'work in a pre-school group' at level 2, and 'family day care' and 'special needs' at level 3. The Local Government Management Board and the Care Sector Consortium have commissioned a study into the feasibility of development and additional endorsement in primary education. The same bodies are currently reviewing the existing units of competence and looking for any significant gaps.

The NVQ standards and qualifications have generally been well received and for many organizations it has been seen as an opportunity for thousands of women to have access to a nationally recognized work-related qualification. It is also regarded as providing improved status and recognition for child-care work and improved standards of child care and education based on nationally agreed criteria for performance in the workplace.

The NVQ standards have also been seen as providing a framework for progression within the workplace or into higher education and professional training. The breadth of the training and the endorsements are also helping to provide early child-care workers with the opportunity to transfer into a wide variety of child-care and education settings.

The Rumbold Committee stated:

> we welcome the work of the National Council for Vocational Qualifications (NCVQ) towards establishing agreed standards for child care workers, including those in educational settings. We believe that, given adequate resourcing, it could bring about significant rationalization of patterns of training. It should also improve the status of early years workers through recognition of the complex range and high levels of skills involved and by opening up prospects for further training.
>
> (DES 1990, para. 176, p. 24)

How popular is the NVQ system?

By the end of 1994 the awarding bodies (CACHE, City and Guilds, B.Tec. and CCETSW) had approved over 300 assessment centres to offer NVQs in child care and education. 'The best practice model' advocated by NCVQ is one involving the setting up of a consortium to include representatives from education, social services, and the private and voluntary sectors. As an external verifier for CACHE I am convinced that these provide all candidates with the most appropriate form of support.

There is considerable interest in NVQs in child care and education but the number of candidates registering has been slower than some people expected. NVQ monitoring in November 1995 showed that there had been

856 candidates who achieved a level 2 qualification and a further 243 have been awarded a level 3 qualification. In the past few months some of the candidates in the voluntary sector have sought and found funding and therefore the number of registrations has risen considerably. The NVQ route is an expensive one for many candidates who are low paid and are frequently self-employed, unlike other occupations where there has been substantial employer support.

Assessment and quality assurance

One of the biggest challenges to the awarding bodies is to ensure that NVQs are truly national standards and that there are not wide-ranging differences up and down the country. Responsibility for ensuring quality and high standards rests predominantly with the internal and external verifiers. These professionals are trained to work with assessors, who may be in the workplace or function as peripatetic assessors. Unlike many other occupations the majority of the candidates are either self-employed, as childminders, or work in very small-scale settings and therefore peripatetic assessors have to be found. One of the difficulties in using peripatetic assessors is the high cost to the candidate as it generally entails a considerable number of visits each of which has to be paid for.

Although NVQs in child care and education are only three years old it seems that the skills and knowledge necessary for child-care workers is reflected in the standards, and most candidates state that registering for their NVQ at either level has resulted in a thorough and rigorous look at their practice in the workplace. This should have a highly positive effect upon the children in their care and their families.

NVQs and children's rights

In this section I want to look at the standards and the assessment procedures and ask whether the children have really gained from the introduction of occupational standards in child care and education. Any procedure which encourages workers to reflect on and evaluate their practice should have a positive effect upon the quality of the care and education they offer.

Close inspection of the various units of competence and the associated performance criteria indicates that they fit well with children's rights. Candidates are expected to demonstrate a thorough knowledge of each of the elements in the units and it is expected that all their work will be underpinned by sound anti-discriminatory practice. Respect for children and their needs is a fundamental tenet of the standards. However, underlying principles and assumptions of the standards must be tested and it is the role of the assessors to probe and investigate the candidate's practice to ensure that the standards of competence have been reached.

Assessment of competence is carried out in a variety of ways. Much of the assessment is based upon direct observation but there are naturally some aspects of practice which need to be assessed by questioning, reflective accounts and other indirect evidence. A particularly sensitive area to assess, but of extreme importance for children's rights, relates to the unit E2.5 'Keep children safe from abuse'. A highly experienced practitioner may be able to respond from personal experience but many candidates will only be able to discuss the situations from a theoretical point of view only.

The assessment procedures in place are sound but they rely upon the skills and knowledge of the assessors – people who must be prepared to state that a candidate is 'not yet competent'. For most candidates in a child-care setting assessment is expensive and it is understandable that a sympathetic assessor may be tempted to accept a lower level of competence if aware of the financial difficulties. However, not only will assessors and verifiers be undermining the standards by adopting a less than rigorous approach but they will also be denying children their rights to quality care and education.

Most assessors and verifiers are impartial and rigorous in their approach, but as the numbers of candidates increase so will the number of assessors and verifiers. Therefore there has to be a tight system of quality assurance to ensure that they all have the knowledge and skills required to assess adequately. Gaining the appropriate qualifications (D32 and 33 for assessors and D34 for internal verifiers) is not enough. Candidates and children will suffer if this new approach is not rigorously and systematically monitored and action is taken against those who fail to maintain the high standards laid down by the National Council for Vocational Qualifications.

Specialist teacher assistants

One of the most recent innovations in training to work with young children is the Specialist Teacher Assistant scheme.

The DFE Circular 14/93 (1993, p. 33) stated that in the near future the first group of specialist teacher assistants (STA) will be joining the workforce. STAs will have undergone a 'rigorous period of study of successful approaches to the teaching of reading, writing, mathematics and of the ways in which classroom assistants can contribute to the teaching and learning of basis skills in support of qualified teachers'.

In March 1994 the Department for Education invited bids for pilot courses which would train classroom assistants in a range of competences related to the exercise of their role under the direction of the teacher. These competences include the development and understanding of:

- the relevant requirements of the primary curriculum;
- the place of the school in educating primary pupils and in promoting the spiritual, moral, social and cultural development of pupils;
- the role of the teacher;

- their own role in relation to teachers, other support staff and agencies, and pupils.

Initially, twenty-six institutions were involved, each offering a different programme of learning and assessment. As the scheme moves into the second year the number of providers has increased to forty. In spite of the initial emphasis upon learning and teaching at Key Stage 1 of the National Curriculum, there is some concern among many providers that the DFEE is placing too great an emphasis upon the knowledge base of mathematics and English at Key Stage 1 and too little attention is being given to *how* children learn, which may not be in the best interests of children. It is certainly in their best interests that there are trained assistants in the classroom to support overworked teachers in large classes but many query whether a rather narrow competency-based approach is necessarily the best way to help foster children's learning and development. It may be that the proposed NVQ endorsement in primary education will provide a more suitable training for classroom assistants.

Recent innovations in training

Among the new initiatives for young people are the general national vocational qualifications (GNVQs) in health and social care. These offer only a very limited range of child-care options, but are proving popular among young people. As they are still in the very early stages of development it is impossible to predict how effective they will be in helping the young people entering to understand and put into practice respect for children's rights.

In a 1994 government white paper the Modern Apprenticeship Scheme was launched. Under this programme young people from 16–19 years could be employed by an organization and attend training and other educational courses to enable them to development core skills and work towards the attainment of NVQ level 3. A few pilot schemes are in existence in child care and education and these are currently being evaluated by consultants at the National Association of Maternal and Child Welfare.

Training in the private sector

Montessori education

Currently there is an increasing interest in Montessori education and in many areas of the UK there is a rapid growth in schools which offer this form of education. There are three main training organizations in the UK which offer either one- or two-year courses to qualify as a Montessori teacher. The DFE does not recognize the qualification as giving teacher status, unlike in the USA where Montessori teachers receive official recognition.

The one-year training course focuses tightly upon the theory and practice of Montessori education for children between the ages of 3 and 6 years, although in at least one of the training institutions student teachers are given an insight into theories of child development and learning and are introduced to issues relating to equal opportunities and anti-discriminatory practices. In this same institution, those students who complete the two-year course focus on the education and needs of children from birth to 3.

One of the major tenets of Montessori philosophy is respect for the child, and a visitor to a true Montessori nursery will see this in action as the child is allowed the freedom to develop at his or her own pace. There is a calmness and serenity in most Montessori nurseries, which is due partly to the philosophy and partly to the fact that the child/adult ratio is 8–1 or less.

Training for work in playgroups

The Preschool Learning Alliance (PLA) encourages as many of its workers as possible to study the Diploma in Playwork Practice. This modular course covers aspects of play and learning, the role of the adult, theories of child development and the business side of running a playgroup, and provides much of the underpinning knowledge for level 3 of the NVQs.

Like other training programmes for working with young children this course covers the major issues concerning children's rights. The PLA provides numerous excellent short courses relating to anti-discriminatory practices and equal opportunities but the focus is often upon the adult's needs and rights, not those of the child.

Are we giving our children a fair deal?

If we look at those rights of children highlighted at the beginning of this chapter and reflect upon the various training programmes available to those who want to work with children in the first eight years of life we can only come to conclusion that no one programme places the child at the centre. All the programmes focus upon how to develop skills and competences for working with young children. In the traditional 'taught courses' there is a strong knowledge element accompanied by practical experience in the workplace, in the NVQ route to training the candidate has to demonstrate competence in the workplace.

Most of the elements necessary to develop a respect for children and their rights are present in all training programmes, but in reality the demands of society force early childhood trainers towards an approach which is not always in the best interests of children. This may be inevitable, but if all early childhood training programmes could include ways of encouraging workers to be advocates for young children then they would at least have the skills to fight for children's rights. Early years workers need to be proactive for the rights and needs of children; the skills needed for this should be practised during training, so that future early childhood workers build up their confidence and motivation to become realistic advocates.

As a country the UK makes inadequate provision for its young children compared with the rest of Europe and other countries in the world. Politicians and government officials point to the increasing number of places available for children under statutory school age. This may be true in some areas of the country, but who is looking to see whether the provision is quality care and education? I return to my initial theme: if high quality education for young children, which is their right, is dependent upon the calibre of the early years provider, then we must make certain that early years training programmes truly respect the rights of the child.

8

Parents and Early Childhood Educators Working Together for Children's Rights

Kath Hirst

This chapter will give examples of ways of working with parents, both in the community and in the nursery, to encourage their involvement in their children's early education. It will acknowledge the role of parents in the education of their young children and discuss the need for nursery staff, headteachers and politicians to value the time spent working with parents. I will make many references to adults, but do so in the context that children's needs, interests and rights are paramount and must not be overridden by the interests of adults – children come first.

We can watch the news on television or read the newspapers and be appalled at how children in our own and other countries are treated. Peter Newell (1991, p. xii) reminds us, however, that this 'should not blind us to the details of our own daily personal relationships with the children we live and work with'. The adoption by the United Nations in November 1989 of the Convention on the Rights of the Child is an opportunity for countries and for each one of us who works with or for children to promote the rights of children.

But if we who work with children are to promote the rights of the child as stated in the Convention, we must be aware of what the Convention is saying. At a recent conference only a handful of teachers had heard of the Convention, so it is with enlightenment in mind that this chapter is written.

Although most of us would agree that all human beings have rights, we may not consider how easy it is for children's rights to be ignored or forgotten. Because they are young they have no voice in our political system and they need support for their rights to be upheld. As Newell (1991) points out, little in the Convention is new as it draws together scattered principles from other conventions and covenants but it does add principles that are pertinent to children. Possibly the two most important are non-discrimination on grounds of race, sex, religion, language, disability, opinion or family background (article 2) and ensuring that adults and organizations consider the best interests of the child when making decisions concerning them (article 3).

The documents on Nursery Education published in January 1996 (SCAA, 1996, p. 7) state: 'Children's experiences at home are highly significant to achievement. Parents significantly influence their children's learning'. If educators accept that parents' attitudes and involvement have a great influence on their children's achievements, we need to consider what educators might mean by parental involvement. David (1990) discusses the three main types of parental involvement as outlined by Torkington (1986): *school-focused*, where parents may be involved in such goals as fund-raising, sports days, fêtes, and so on; *curriculum-focused*, where parents are involved in developing children's cognitive skills; and *parent-focused*, which gives parents the opportunity to know and understand their own children's learning and development of their own skills and confidence. Torkington sees this third approach as the one closest to partnership as it starts with the assumption that parents know their child best.

Braun (1992, p. 180), however, summarizes my view of a model of working with parents:

> It is about recognising that partnership is needed in order to benefit the child; that both partners bring equal but different skills to the task; that both need to listen, learn and change accordingly. Parents have a detailed and intimate knowledge of their child; staff know about children and their development. Both sets of skills and knowledge are vital for each child to achieve her full potential.

However, as Braun points out, different parents will bring different experiences, expectations and varying degrees of confidence. What works with one set of parents may need a different approach with a 'new' set of parents. It is an ongoing process that needs to be constantly reviewed as new parents voice their preferences and concerns or as new approaches are tried.

The School Curriculum and Assessment Authority identifies parents' role as a significant feature of good practice: 'Parents' fundamental role in their child's education is acknowledged by staff in the setting and a partnership, based on shared responsibility, understanding, mutual respect and dialogue, is developed' (SCAA, 1996, p. 7).

Parents as partners

The government consultation document *Preschool Education* (SCAA, 1995) included several references to parents, including a section called 'Parents as Partners', and states the value of parents and providers working together to support children's learning, asserting that 'the results have a measurable and lasting effect upon their [children's] achievement' (ibid.). The document suggested that success depended on a two-way flow of opportunities for knowledge, expertise and information and summarised the following common key features underlying effective partnerships of parents and providers involved in children's education:

- parents' fundamental role in their child's education is acknowledged by staff in the setting;
- there is recognition of the role parents have already played in the early education of their children and that their continued involvement is crucial to successful learning;
- parents feel welcome in the setting and there are opportunities for collaboration between the parent, provider and the child;
- there is recognition of the expertise of parents and other adults in the family and this expertise is used to support the learning opportunities provided within the setting;
- providers give parents access to information about the curriculum in a variety of ways, e.g. open days, meetings, social events, video presentations, brochures;
- parents are kept fully informed of their child's progress and achievements;
- admission procedures are flexible to allow time for discussion with parents and for children to feel secure in the new setting;
- opportunities for learning provided in the setting are sometimes continued at home, e.g. home reading links, and experiences at home are sometimes used as stimuli for learning in the setting.

(SCAA, 1995, p. 14)

Four detailed examples of effective partnerships were given as guidance:

- a parent sharing a book with a small group of children;
- a visit from a mother who was a doctor – stimulating imaginative role play;
- a father who was a gardening expert brought produce from his allotment and talked about his gardening with the children;
- a mother brought her new baby to the group, prompting discussion about christenings and families.

The final document *Nursery Education* (SCAA, 1996) asserts the place of parental involvement in early learning in nurseries and other early childhood groups. I want now to examine some ways in which working with parents in the spirit of the SCAA document, and in a wider sense, might influence children's rights.

Working together to protect children

When writing about working with parents we must always be aware that there are instances when it seems that some parents do not have the best interests of their children at heart. We hear of sexual and physical abuse of children by one of their parents. What we can do in these circumstances is to support children and parents and work with other professionals to help families work through these situations, which are often exacerbated by other circumstances such as poverty, unemployment and low self-esteem. Although a child may not be subject to physical or sexual abuse, emotional abuse such as witnessing domestic violence is confusing and upsetting to children, and can be damaging too.

A nursery child was absolutely distraught as he watched another child kick and stamp on a ladybird. When the tears subsided he managed to explain between sobs that the incident had reminded him of something that had happened at home. These instances should not be tucked away and ignored after the tears subside. It is our role as professionals to support the child and family, involving other professionals where necessary. Family and financial circumstances were causing excessive stress in this little boy's life. As a result of nursery staff listening to his father, steps were taken to alleviate the situation and the child's level of stress was eased. Newell (1991) emphasizes the need for the state and all professionals to help reduce stress in families which could lead to physical or emotional abuse of children. There is a need to be proactive in detecting the underlying causes of abuse and thereby introducing preventive measures.

In another instance, a child who had witnessed domestic violence and was subjected to emotional abuse was, understandably, finding settling into nursery a traumatic experience. Although nursery staff could appreciate his mother's need to leave him, as she was on her own with six children, in the best interests of the child she or another adult he could trust needed to stay until he was settled. By talking with the family it was agreed that either his mother or his aunt, whom he trusted, would stay even though the settling-in period took three weeks. He became a contented child in nursery as he gradually realized, with the help of his family and nursery staff, that he was in a safe and secure environment where he was free to investigate, explore and make sense of this new part of his world.

Enriching experiences

Financial constraints and poverty can seriously affect children's lives. This is discussed in a study by Bradshaw (1990), where families who were dependent on benefit commented how their children did not get any treats, did not have many clothes and did not go anywhere. Involving parents in both local visits to places of interest and visits further afield to the coast, the countryside or to working farms can create a new interest for all the family which can help to alleviate the negative constraints incurred by poverty.

Hirst and Hannon (1990) report in a study of a Sheffield home-teaching project, how low-income parents remarked that visits had been particularly enjoyable and beneficial to their children. Parents commented how their children had talked for days about their experiences, and some families visited places of interest again on their own. Athey's work (1990), and later that of Nutbrown (1994a) showed the importance of professionals working with parents and children together in the wider environment.

In one of the multi-ethnic nurseries where I have worked, a nursery visit to a farm prompted parents of Asian origin to share their childhood experiences of rural life in Pakistan with their children and with nursery staff. Many had been brought up in the rural area around Rawal Pindi and some of the children's grandparents still lived there. They were delighted to send photographs of their involvement in school life in the UK to their extended family in Pakistan. As one older sister explained, 'Parents are not expected to be involved in their child's education in Pakistan.' Respect for one another's cultures upholds article 29(1)c, which states:

> the education of the child shall be directed to:
> . . . the development of respect for the child's parents, his or her own cultural identity, language and values, for the national values of the country in which the child is living, the country from which he or she may originate, and for civilisations different from his or her own.

Acknowledging and celebrating festivals from different faiths and cultures develops an awareness of similarities and differences between cultures and religions. Mothers come into nursery to help prepare food for Eid parties, bringing a taste of their traditional food for all the children to share. Throughout the year they will help with preparation of food for snacks which will reflect their culture. While they are working in the nursery, staff will explain and demonstrate the philosophy of learning through play.

One Asian mother who was not quite sure how to play with her child at the dough table observed a member of staff rolling, cutting, patting, and stretching the dough, talking to the children as she was playing. The mother then introduced something of her own culture by rolling and patting the dough to make chapatis with her two children, talking to them all the time in Punjabi. The children then shared the chapatis with their teacher.

Children hearing their home language in the nursery creates familiarity, values the home language and shows the parents that staff and school respect their community. For children who speak English as their home language the experience of hearing another language in an everyday context is enriching too. As Siraj-Blatchford (1994, p. 45) points out: 'young children need to have their languages valued and their home experiences affirmed in order to venture into the language and culture of the early years setting'.

Home visiting

Nursery Education – Desirable Outcomes for Children's Learning and Guidance for Providers refers mainly to work with parents in group settings, though they do acknowledge parents' 'fundamental role in their child's education' (SCAA, 1996 p. 7). Working with parents in their own home adds another dimension to partnership with parents. To ensure that the best needs of children are met, most children in the multicultural nursery I am describing here are visited at home before they enter nursery. Our approach to home visiting is based on non-judgemental attitudes and the development of good relationships based on mutual trust and acceptance. Parents are contacted before the visit to make the necessary arrangements and also to give them the opportunity to refuse if they so wish. Very few parents refuse such invitations. Those that do usually refuse because they are working and so call into the nursery at a time which is convenient to them, or the child visits with his or her carer.

Home visits enable staff, parents and children to meet in the security of the child's home, and parents share with staff their first-hand knowledge of the child. Toys, books photographs and the nursery booklet are taken by the staff to share with the family. Where necessary, a member of the nursery staff who can translate will accompany the key worker. This key worker system provides a contact person whom both the child and the parent(s) have met prior to entry into nursery. In a busy nursery this is a good support system and point of contact for parents and children. The key worker is usually the person who then works with the parent or carer to settle the child into nursery.

Home visiting and early literacy

Another approach to home visiting was initiated in the same nursery. This was a short-term project over two terms consisting of more frequent home visits before children started nursery. It was partly funded by the OMEP (UK) Children's Fund, the UK part of the World Organization for Early Childhood Education, an organization dedicated to promoting quality of life for young children. Our aims were to get to know the families of pre-nursery children or to build on existing relationships and to focus on young children's literacy development in families of Asian origin. The project was based on the belief that, as Hannon (1995, p. 50) states, 'parents are a highly motivated teaching force and schools should not allow their potential to be wasted'. In addition, 'much literacy – perhaps most – is learnt at home . . . and that involvement is feasible, rewarding, and can help meet the goals of schools and families' (ibid., p. 151).

All the parents of children due to start nursery the following term were asked whether they would like staff to visit on a fortnightly basis. All parents accepted, a clear message that this group of people wanted to work together to the benefit of their children. We recognized that parents' experiences of education, either in the UK or in Pakistan, varied greatly. Some parents, as in the home-teaching project previously mentioned (Hirst and Hannon, 1990), had received little or no education at school, some had memories of unpleasant experiences, others had positive experiences and outcomes.

Some parents and children did not speak English; Mirpuri Punjabi or Urdu was their first language. In other homes parents and/or children spoke some English, while in some homes both children and parents spoke English. Most families had Mirpuri Punjabi (which does not have a written form) as their first language. In some homes parents could read English and Urdu or English and Bengali, some read only in their home language or only in English and some parents did not read at all.

During the preliminary visit the literacy home background (as outlined above) was established in order to ensure a sensitive approach. Books, writing materials and photographs of everyday nursery events and activities were taken into the homes by nursery staff. Visits were planned by the teacher and the bilingual child-care assistant who also acted as interpreter. In most of the homes children had access to some books and mark-making materials. During the visits books and photographs were shared with the families and children were given opportunities for mark-making. If children had their own books they would share those with parents, siblings, the extended family or nursery staff. Books and writing materials were left in the home in a wallet which proved to be very special to the child. On the next home visit, parents would discuss their child's interest in the books and the child would proudly share his or her drawings.

We found a positive interest in books and book-sharing in all the families. Many of the books provided by nursery were picture books, so if parents could not read it was still possible to share the book in their home language by using the pictures. Although parents were very busy and some had large families to cook for, they and the extended family usually found time to share the books and writing materials and welcomed our visits. Older children who could read also shared the books with their younger brothers and sisters, delightedly telling us at school how they had been reading at home, so the interest in early literacy was extended to older children also.

The parents were asked to encourage careful book-handling skills, starting at the opposite end for English books from those written in Urdu and encouraging the children to turn the pages one at a time. Good relationships were established and maintained. Families new to school were met in their own homes (less threatening than at school) and children established positive beginnings with nursery staff.

Parents were also invited to bring their young children to the toddler group which was held in the community room in school. Books and mark-making materials were once more available along with other toys and activities. Parents and children had the opportunity to meet one another in a friendly school environment; they then came through into nursery for the last half-hour of the session.

Parents were very positive about the project as the following comments demonstrate:

> It's so nice that you come to visit us at home before children go to school. In Pakistan you just have to take them and leave them. Adnan liked the book about nursery. He said he was in the story and Zain [the baby]). He is pretending to write now.
>
> (Mother of 2-year-old (translated from Punjabi))

> His older brothers and sisters read to him. He likes to sit at the side of his older brothers when they are doing their homework or when I am teaching them Urdu. He pretends to write too.
>
> (Father of 2-year- old)

> I like the books in Urdu and English. I can read it in Urdu and then explain to her in Punjabi. The older children will learn Urdu through this book as well. Her sister will tell her the words in English.
>
> (Mother of 2-year-old-girl)

These comments from parents illustrate the literacy and oracy environment in the home. They also illustrate the attitudes of parents to early literacy and the early attitudes of 2-year-olds to books and early reading and writing. There was a shared knowledge of the children from the people who know them best and a trusting partnership developed through the project.

In an ideal world the project would have continued but time and staffing constraints made this impossible, and so, like many initiatives that benefit children and their families, this sustained and systematic involvement was curtailed. However, home visits are still made on a more restricted basis and parents are still invited to the toddler group which is now held in the nursery. Parents and children are also invited to participate in the toy library and book library each week.

Conclusion

In her book about the development of the Pen Green Centre for Under-Fives and their Families, Whalley (1994) tells the story of how staff, parents and children worked together to set up and develop this unique centre. It is a story of mutual respect, of learning and continuing to learn so that the interests of the community the centre serves are always held in focus and an illustration of what can happen when rights are respected and real partnerships are created.

If children's rights are to be upheld, professional educators and parents need to acknowledge the role that they play in enabling the voices of children to be heard. If parents are welcome and we as educators work in partnership to ensure their participation, with understanding, in their children's education, the best needs of the children will be met without discrimination on grounds of 'race, sex, religion, language, disability, opinion or family background' (article 2). Pugh, De'Ath and Smith (1994) argue the need for education and support for parents in their 'Agenda for Action'. They argue that support in the form of a range of schemes and services available in a local area is necessary to help parents to fulfil their responsibilities as set out in the Children Act 1989, and to enable them to enjoy their children.

Some LEAs have section 11 funded staff who work with ethnic minority children. Their involvement alongside mainstream staff ensures that the best needs of ethnic minority children are met. Such additional funding is constantly under threat of cutbacks and the future of these essential services is insecure. The outcomes of these reductions in services may well place the development of the UN Convention on the Rights of the Child in jeopardy in terms of equal opportunities for *all* children.

All children should have a right to high quality nursery education from adults trained to degree level or equivalent (see chapter 7). As I have already discussed, *preschool* education is now under debate and government is to decide on policy. Whatever the outcome, quality provision which supports the rights of the child must be promoted and maintained. Such provision must incorporate ways that promote partnership with parents not simply through documentation and rhetoric but through adequate resourcing, staff development and support. By such means we may see the effective implementation of new policies that are in tune with the UN Convention on the Rights of the Child and the best of current practice.

9

Their Right to Play

Tricia David

The right to play and recreation

Article 31 of the UN Convention on the Rights of the Child calls for all children to have 'rest and leisure, to engage in play and recreational activities appropriate to the age of the child' (UN, 1989). That this statement had to be made is an indication that there are some children in the world who do not enjoy these rights.

Perhaps we may feel the article is directed not at countries like our own but at those where very young children work in factories, unprotected by laws governing safety or hours and conditions, or countries where malnutrition is so rife that children are too weak and debilitated to have the energy to want play, and the search for food becomes the only object in life, or countries where children are still traded as slaves for work including prostitution.

In the UK we may pride ourselves on having eradicated young children's labour in the mines, mills and chimneys long ago, but with what kind of directed activity and/or drudgery have we replaced this for some? Article 31, after all, does not say children must play all their waking hours, and what constitutes play? Are children who are driven to and from school or nursery, then swept on a tide of gym classes, swimming lessons and horse-riding playing during those sessions? And are the hours taken up by television and computer games regarded as leisure by the children themselves and would they be better spent outdoors in a mixed-age group, using the twigs and leaves of children past as their playthings (Thompson, 1945; Humphreys, Mack and Perks, 1988)? Are the children whose parents cannot afford the organized classes losing out or are they wise to argue that 'they are only little once, let them enjoy their childhood'? Certainly Scandinavian research would suggest that both extremes mean disadvantages for the children involved; a balance would be better (Dahlberg, 1991; Hallden, 1991). In both Western and Eastern European countries there are those who express their fears for the growing generations of children who are not allowed to play out because of the lack of safe, accessible, open spaces. The result is limited access to children's culture and to opportunities for learning about nurturing those who are smaller and weaker than oneself (Hillman, Adams and Whitelegg, 1990; and see papers in David and Nutbrown, 1993).

Additionally, the advent of the National Curriculum with testing at 7 has made parents of 4-year-olds anxious about play methods in nurseries and playgroups (David, 1992b) and the majority of 4-year-olds are in school, with well over half being in the reception classes of primary schools rather than in early childhood provision (Central Statistical Office, 1995). Although many teachers in reception classes have worked hard to provide play activities and a nursery-style setting for those children, is the formality reported in research literature (for example, Bennet and Kell 1989; Drummond, 1995) and by HMI (DES, 1989; OFSTED, 1994) really so bad? Why do nursery practitioners believe a curriculum based on play is superior to one where children are taught formally, with teacher-directed work, by the transmission method? Compared to some of the ills, such as homelessness, abuse, war and famine, affecting the lives of children, does this really matter?

The pioneers of the play curriculum

Jean-Jacques Rousseau (1712–78) advocated a curriculum for the young based on nature and discovery learning. The extent of his influence, following the publication of *Émile* in 1762 should not be underestimated. As with other, earlier writers and theorists such as Comenius, who lived in the fifteenth century, one can trace the web of connections over time and space and it is exciting to reflect on the ways in which we ourselves are influenced by ideas and beliefs about the world which appeal to us because they seem to fit the context in which we find ourselves and match the explanations towards which we are groping.

Robert Owen (1771–1858) had plenty of opportunities to see the effects of harsh lives and repetitive work on the bodies and minds of growing children, through his factory experience in Manchester and New Lanarkshire. He came to the conclusion that factory owners should provide decent housing for workers and schools for children, so that those aged up to 7 spent most of their day in dancing, movement and play.

At around the same time, in other parts of Europe, Pestalozzi and Froebel were developing their influential ideas and putting them into practice. Later, Maria Montessori was to formulate her theories, which have also had a long-standing impact upon early years practice in the UK. Later, Margaret McMillan and Susan Isaacs were further to develop the earlier visions, despite the fact that they had been working in very different contexts – Isaacs in a prestigious, well-endowed nursery in

Cambridge, Macmillan in areas of extreme poverty in Bradford and Deptford.

Later significant influences on the early years curriculum and thinking about children's learning include Jean Piaget, with whom Susan Isaacs was in regular correspondence until her death in 1946. Piaget's work was interpreted as indicating that children needed time to play and investigate their environment free of the demands of adult intervention, and that in any case the stages in cognitive development were fixed, so there was no point in rushing children on and confusing them with concepts they simply could not understand.

Despite Isaacs's (1929) clear recognition of young children's powers, perhaps her too early departure from the field meant that there were few counters to the theories and research prevalent in developmental psychology until the late 1970s. That ethos acted as a barrier to knowledge about young children. It tended to be negative, about what young children could not do rather than the amazing extent of their competence. Advances since then show young children to be active inquirers into their world, who are methodical and self-regulated in that inquiry (Deloache and Brown, 1987).

Research by the post-Piagetians (e.g. Donaldson, 1978) and Jerome Bruner's work (e.g. 1977, 1990), together with Vygotsky's theory (1978) about the social nature of learning, and evidence from the field of psycho-biology (Trevarthen, 1992a), has led to a view of young children as people who are born predisposed to try actively to make sense of the cultural context into which they arrive. We can help that learning process by offering relevant, meaningful and challenging activities and to do this we have a responsibility to try to see the world from the child's point of view.

What this means is that we must reflect constantly on our provision – the setting (indoors and out), the equipment, the people, the 'tasks', the styles of interaction – asking ourselves why the provision was thus and what happened as a result, if it was meaningful to the children, and whether we are able to indicate what learning went on.

Whatever we may feel about the nature of early childhood and whatever research has demonstrated about young children's ability to be active, the rationale for the play tradition will be sustained only if we are able to give reasoned arguments about its value and efficacy.

What sort of play should we be ensuring?

Jamie has big eyes as he looks round the large classroom that he has been attending for the last month. He was 4 in June and now it is October and he is in 'big school'. He and the other fourteen children in his 'group' are examining the various items laid out for them in this quadrant of the room. In the other three quadrants there are three more 'groups' of fifteen children doing other activities, some at tables, and in one area there is a home corner constructed as well as the staff could manage with the meagre resources available. There are two teachers and two classroom assistants and each is responsible for an area of the room. After a while struggling with a jigsaw he can make neither head nor tail of, Jamie finds a box in which there are assorted, interesting items. He wants to handle them, to feel the sleek surface of the big cowrie shell which comfortably fills his small hand, put its smooth, hard, shiny back against his cheek but, just as he begins, a tambourine is shaken and all the children are in a hubbub. Jamie looks at the visitor who has been sitting in the corner, his eyes filling with tears, but he smiles bravely and says in a quavering voice 'I think it's funny when we have to do this.' He moves away, at the centre of his little 'herd', to the next quadrant.

In another school, Lee stands at the sand tray and surveys the rest of the room. The head and the teacher and governors know the arrangement is not ideal for 4-year-olds, and the school cannot afford extra help in this vertically grouped infant class in a two-teacher village school. So the teacher must cope alone with twenty-one children aged between 4 and 7. Lee plays for a while, the teacher glancing around occasionally to be aware of everything that is going on, while concentrating on one particular group of children and their learning. She has organized the room so that the children can be as independent as possible, with areas where they can choose toys and equipment from the clearly marked shelves and then return them. When Lee ends his play at the sand – a familiar and secure base at which to start his day – he picks up the notebook and pencil which are attached to the sand tray by a string and leaves a 'note', a record that he, Lee, played in the sand, that he filtered it through a fine sieve and noticed the tiny pieces of cracked sea shell that were left behind. That is what he tells the teacher his writing is about when they look at the notebook together later. Lee knows that the other children do this, make a record, talk about what they found out, what they think and know about it. He also knows that the notes are meaningful, that he can make his own record, that he is an interesting, powerful person whose play is important to the adults in his life.

In a nursery school, Zaheda shares a bilingual story book with Sam. They are laughing together and making eye-contact; their affection for each other, their joy in being together, is palpable. When they have finished they drift over to the home corner, arm in arm. But then Sam notices the nursery assistant has some fruit on a table, she's waiting to see who will choose to join her, though she has in mind one or two children she would like to involve too. Zaheda asks what they are going to do. The nursery nurse explains they are going to look at the fruit and do some drawings from close observation, then they will use the fruit to make a salad for everyone. 'Will we cut them open to do drawings like we did with the vegetables? I did the broad beans in the pod, like little people in a soft bed', says Sam. They are told the fruit will eventually be cut open. Sam points to a mango and inquires what it is. This makes Zaheda ask Sam if she knows what colour the mango fruit is on the inside. She laughs when Sam says she doesn't know, and tells her to guess. 'You'll just have to see, won't you?' Zaheda retorts, with a loving, knowing laugh.

There can be many reasons for the provision of play opportunities in early childhood settings. They may include social learning device, cognitive learning device, physical learning device, fun/freedom, therapy, and occupation while the adults direct other groups or individuals. In the anecdotes above, it is probable that all the episodes would be labelled as play by the children involved, yet their experiences were very different and very variable in their capacity to engender learning.

Observational studies of young children in group settings (Sylva, Roy and Painter, 1980; Hutt *et al.*, 1989) have led to the conclusion that child-directed play which is intrinsically challenging needs to be the goal of early years providers. A resort to too much adult direction or too much *laissez-faire* can both reduce this challenge. In a more recent contemporary project Liz Smith and Neville Bennett (1995) are finding that many early years teachers are unable to articulate exactly what a child is gaining from a play activity, and it may be fear of this 'unknown' which makes practitioners take up the extreme ends of the spectrum – one moment being overly directing and setting tasks, the next expecting children to 'play' without any involvement from the adults.

According to Hutt *et al.* (1989), nursery teachers involved during their project were reluctant to use the term exploration for 'play' where the children are investigating and experimenting through touching, manipulating, smelling, tasting, listening to and looking at materials or other aspects of their environment. This exploratory phase can be quite easily discerned from the truly playful phase which the project decided to call 'ludic' (from Berlyne, 1970). As they state, the ludic phase has what Miller (1973) called its 'gallumphing' quality – the fun, shared laughter, funny voices, and so on. What should also be added about it is that it has no apparent 'pay-off', no new learning happens in this phase, but the child uses new learning and gains confidence and control, metaphorically asking the question 'What can I do with this?' This play follows bouts of exploratory learning called 'epistemic play', when the behaviour is goal-orientated, purposeful and more serious, as witnessed by facial expressions and language. In epistemic play children are metaphorically asking the question 'What does this do?' of a material or object, or even of a person or other living creature. 'Free-play, or ludic activity, clearly has an important role in psychological development, but it requires appropriate counterbalancing by epistemic activity' (Hutt *et al.*, 1989, p. 226).

Similarly, Janet Moyles (1989) indicates how adults can intervene in the 'play spiral', helping children access the learning they want to achieve, scaffolding that learning, providing for new challenges the children indicate and then withdrawing to allow space for further epistemic and ludic episodes. Both phases are enjoyable. That enjoyment, choosing an activity freely because of its appeal rather than having it imposed by someone with more power, is one aspect of the definition of play but the style of the enjoyment is different in the two phases. Anyone who has struggled to find out about or make something will know the great sense of exhilaration on achieving success – it is very different from the enjoyment and relaxation involved in 'having a good laugh with friends'. Both have an important place in fulfilled lives.

Learning is serious stuff

Perhaps the problem is that we in the UK live in an ethos of the Protestant work ethic and this has been exacerbated by the recession. Education seems to have become subject to those who think that if it isn't hurting it isn't working. Our education system has been blamed for Britain's failure to keep up with competitors and we are constantly told that 'better-educated' recruits are required by industry and commerce. What we need to ask is, in what sense should the recruits be more able, and what is education for – only to satisfy industrial needs or, as the Warnock Report (DES, 1978) recommended, for the individual's own life enrichment as well as enabling each person to contribute to society? Play, because of its enjoyable qualities and control by the player/child, is not seen as contributing to serious learning.

Only recently has the powerful influence of the emotions on learning been acknowledged, after all, rationalists, believing in the Age of Enlightenment's split between body and mind, emotion and reason, hang on to their claim of a potentially logical view of life and the world, while the postmodernists attempt to take centre stage stressing the fractured nature of this supposed new era. I would argue that the field of early childhood and those who work with small children have always had problems with the limited nature of rationality, because early childhood involves so much more openly the imperatives of emotions and bodily functions. This is not to say young children and their educators cannot be rational, only that 'pure' rationalists behave as if the tip of the iceberg *were* the iceberg. The Age of Enlightenment brought many benefits, but it also eroded people's contact with the land and the rhythms of the seasons and cycles of life. Now, with new forms of technology and travel, we may be moving still further from nature and its cyclical rhythms.

Yet some colleagues (e.g. Bailey, forthcoming) are returning to arguments about the basic biological imperative for play experiences for young children, in the way that young animals appear to need these. We are slowly realizing our responsibility to the earth and that harmony with nature, the premodern view, rather than the rationalist attempts to subjugate nature and the earth, is crucial to our survival. Will a similar conclusion dawn upon us in relation to babies and children?

In the interim, the idea that learning is indeed a serious business, but one which can be experienced as enjoyable and fun, is difficult to convey to those who believe formality, efficiency and content prescription ensure learning. Perhaps the very idea that something so serious as learning about the world and how to live could be best achieved by being enjoyable, largely self-directed and controlled by the learner, even when – especially when – that learner is a small child, is something of a paradox for those of a Puritanical frame of mind.

> David started nursery after spending the daytime hours of the three years he had been in this world in his parents' hairdressing salon. For the first few weeks he played in a solitary fashion for much of the time, arranging chairs in an arc, sitting all the dolls and teddies he could gather on them and talking to his 'customers'. His teacher and nursery nurse could tell he was talking to them because they could see his lips moving, but whenever they or another child came too close, David would stop, stand still and stare at the 'intruder'. The teacher and nursery nurse could see that, among other things, David was capable of – matching one-to-one, sequencing (the attention he gave his customers showed that) and putting objects (the 'customers' and other items he used) into sets. All of this, however, was not their concern at that time. They recognized that David needed to continue with this activity – the best match to his familiar everyday experiences he could get in this strange new place with so many children instead of lots of adults. The nursery staff also recognized his need for time and were rewarded when he gradually allowed or invited other children to share his play, then to involve (and direct) an adult, and eventually to leave this activity, no longer needing it, except when his expert input was required in the setting up of a dramatic play hair salon.

Learning in the culture

Sutton-Smith (1979) argues that play is used by societies to prepare children for life in that context and in some societies may even be a way of fostering conformity. In the 1970s, studies such as those by King (1978) and Sharp and Green (1975), and later by Tizard and Hughes (1984), exposed the failure of some early years teachers to adapt to the needs of individual children, to recognize the fact that some children have learnt from their families how to access an informal curriculum, with its invisible structure, while other children are denied this because their parents have not been enabled to understand the meaning of learning through play.

Sutton-Smith's (1979) view is endorsed by the research carried out by Sally Lubeck (1986). She adopted the role of participant observer in two early years groups in a city in the USA. One nursery was situated in a poor Afro-American community, the other in an advantaged 'white' suburb. In each group there were three women workers but their interactions with one another and with the children in their groups were significantly different. In one, children were learning to be individualistic and competitive, in the other co-operative and supportive. Even adult–adult interactions reflected these different types of ethos, so the role modelling by the adults reinforced the styles the children were learning in their play. What is sad is that both groups could have learned from each other – almost like Western and Eastern Europeans sharing learning about individualism and sense of community as aspects of democracy. After all, there are times in our lives when we have to be brave enough to dare to do things on our own but we also need to be capable of accepting and giving support – to understand the strengths of interdependence.

Play as a mode of expressing views, wishes and feelings

The Children Act 1989 demands that children's views be heard and taken into account. Since a number of other countries have recently passed similar legislation, one can trace a link with the UN Convention. The language needed to express actively some of their innermost wishes or fears may be too complex for very young children. They may be unable to put their feelings into words because they have been forbidden to tell anyone, or at least consider they do not have 'permission' to divulge something secret and frightening. Play can be the way in which children find an outlet for the expression of these anxieties. This may manifest itself in almost any type of play provision, for example during a bout of pretend play, or in painting, or playing with clay, with dolls, and so on. The right of a child to live without fear of abuse may depend upon the expertise of an educator who identifies and 'hears' such a cry for help. Play therefore provides for young children's emotional well-being, as well as for their physical, social and cognitive development.

Adults and play: living to play or playing to live?

Charles Handy's (1994) *The Empty Raincoat* and articles about work hours (DEMOS, 1995) demonstrate how adults who are in full-time, paid employment are beginning to realize that their work is creating barriers between them and those with whom they have the most meaningful relationships in their lives. For the UK employed, work is taking up too much time.

Meanwhile, those who are unemployed and living in poverty would willingly give up some of their time for a share of the earnings of the employed. They have plenty of free time but little opportunity to spend that time as they would wish. Even taking on an allotment in order to grow one's own food is out of reach of most in this group, because, while the rents for allotments are modest, they cannot afford the costs of buying seeds, tools, and so on.

As Handy (1994) argues, some have money and no time, some time but no money. The result is a society which is ill at ease with itself. Children are experiencing poor role models through being with adults who have either too little time for them, or too little patience and resources to be capable of appropriate engagement. Perhaps community feeling might re-emerge if people could afford to invest time and money in local leisure activities, including those with and for children. The African proverb says 'It takes a village to educate a child.'

The UN Convention article 31 uses the word 'recreation' – if we write this as re-creation, it is possible to see how leisure, time to 'play' and to 'be', is meant to be renewing, a time to create ourselves afresh, transform ourselves. For young children, who are 'new' anyway, play offers a way of participating in decisions about their own 'creation'. If children's time and activities are constantly determined and organized by the adults in their lives, how can they ever explore answers to their own questions about the world and about themselves? They are playing to live.

10

Questions for Respectful Educators

Cathy Nutbrown

In the opening chapter Gerison Lansdown posed some questions. This final chapter reviews contributions in relation to article 29 of the UN Convention and looks forward to progress on children's rights in the new millennium, posing yet more questions.

The early 1990s witnessed an ongoing debate in Britain about day care and education for our youngest children. Cases have been made about different kinds of provision: voluntarily run playgroups argued that they were best placed to provide for the non-statutory age group; private nurseries grew and promoted themselves as the most flexible service for working parents; state nursery classes and nursery schools continued to assert that they offered the most appropriate kind of curriculum, built on a tradition of good practice and linked into the later educational expectations of the National Curriculum; childminders stated that they offered the most personal and responsive service to parents. The debate therefore involved voluntary, private and state providers.

There was an unfortunate subtext about this debate that seemed to revolve around issues like which service was 'best' and should therefore receive government funding and endorsement. The Early Childhood Education Forum was formed amid this debate, under the umbrella of the National Children's Bureau and chaired by Dr Gillian Pugh. This was an attempt to find common ground from which to take forward the case for quality in early childhood education, whatever the setting.

Speculation was rife throughout 1994 and early 1995 while the government appeared to ponder on its policy and its commitment to under-5s provision and then, in July 1995, announced a decision to provide parents of 4-year-old children with a voucher with which they can purchase some form of 'education'. Consultation documents – *Desirable Outcomes for Children's Learning*, and *'Light touch' Inspection* of 'education' for 4-year-olds

– were issued in September 1995 (SCAA, 1995; DFEE/DOH, 1995; DFEE, 1995) and final documentation published in January 1996 (SCAA 1996, DFEE 1996). Within this climate various claims and counterclaims were being made about the different types of provision. There was discussion about the immediate benefits, long-term benefits and, uppermost in the minds of those who watch the purse strings, the term 'value for money'. The Audit Commission for England and Wales carried out a study into nursery education (1994–5) and examined different types of provision in order to study, among other things, resources, local authority strategy, the length of time children spend in each setting, and assessment of the effectiveness of different experiences and types of experiences. The principal objective was to consider how to make the best use of resources rather than to recommend what the overall level of provision should be or what constituted 'good' or 'bad' practice (Audit Commission, 1994).

A climate of competition rather than collaboration existed between providers and advocates of particular types of provision and, at times, gave the feeling that organizations and agencies were there to perpetuate their own existence rather than to further the cause for which they were first established – namely to provide opportunities for young children to play and learn. There are vast differences in inspections of provision for under-5s, with LEA nursery schools and classes being subjected to the rigour of OFSTED inspection every four years and playgroups, creches, private nurseries and childminders having to comply with the more health and safety orientated, annual inspection required in the Children Act 1989 (see chapter 2 and Pugh, 1992). The qualifications and experience of OFSTED and Children Act inspectors vary tremendously as do the criteria for inspection and the detail of the reports. Moves in 1995 to 'marry' OFSTED and Children Act inspections were welcomed from the point of view of sensibility but there were some worries that the rigour of inspections of nursery schools and classes may be lost. If they were inspected by different criteria and processes the status of their inspections as already discussed by Jean Ensing (chapter 2) could be reduced, they may be marginalized from other forms of education in the school system and the development of positive experiences for young children could be threatened in a watering down or levelling out of all forms of 'under-5s' provision rather than achieving high quality across the spectrum.

The jumble of provision gives the illusion of choice and diversity but in reality presents an unhelpful situation for parents making decisions about forms of early education and care and masks the reality of a lack of provision. How do parents and early childhood educators make decisions about quality of provision?

I want to suggest here that one way of deciding whether a provision is 'good enough' for children, whatever the label might be, is to examine it in terms of children's rights – although currently such issues are not overtly included in inspection criteria for day-care or education settings in the UK. The concept of 'good enough' is borrowed from Pugh, De'Ath and Smith (1994) – who follow in the footsteps of Winnicott and Bettleheim. They write about the concept of 'good enough' or confident parenting. I use the terms here to refer to the level of quality that should be expected in any provision for children under 5. I suggest that for any provision to be 'good enough for children', good enough for the 'confident mark', it must embrace the rights of the child. The contributors to this book have asserted their belief that the whole of the UN Convention is important, and have focused on different articles in the Convention and what they may mean for educators. In this chapter I shall look at the way in which article 29 might be interpreted for children under 5. Peter Newell (1991) has examined UK legislation in terms of the UN Convention and found it wanting. The Children's Rights Development Unit's (1994) *Agenda for Children* has detailed the state of play for children and their rights in the UK (see chapter 1). Children's rights, however, are the responsibility of everyone, not simply of the government of the day. Every educator, indeed every adult citizen, must come to realize that they as well as government have a responsibility to work for children's rights and that they can do much on a day-to-day basis to support, extend and uphold children's rights.

I will take each section of article 29 and pose some questions about how early childhood educators might have regard to this part of the Convention. These questions can be used by practitioners to examine their own nurseries and other forms of provision in terms of children's rights to see if it reaches the 'confident mark'. In relation to each subsection of article 29 I will discuss what the realities for some children in nurseries and other forms of early provision might be. Though provision for children under 5 is not a legal requirement and parents do not have to send their children to nurseries (or to school until the term after they are five), it is important to see how educators might respect children in terms of this part of the Convention as well as asserting here the right of children, from birth, to opportunities to learn, to care, to education, to *educaré*. That may be at home, with parents or other family members, it may, for some of the time, be in group or other home settings. Wherever they find themselves children should receive respect from responsible, knowledgeable, responsive and sensitive adults.

Article 29a

The development of the child's personality, talents and mental and physical abilities to their fullest potential.

- How does the provision foster the development of individuals, their personality, their talents, their thinking and their actions to the fullest?
- Do educators observe and discuss the personalities and preferences of the children they work with – babies, toddlers, and older children?
- Do the children work on challenging problems?

> - Do they confront issues which puzzle and bother them?
> - How can a service for children foster healthy hearts and minds?
> - Do educators challenge children to stretch themselves or do they train children to conform?

Children are born poised to learn. They are eager to do, know, think, understand. *Real understanding* is a process of discovery and if we want *real learning* we must create the kinds of conditions in which discoveries are made. Children must have time, freedom, space, lack of pressure, as well as real challenge, using the 'stuff' of which the world is made – clay, sand, water – and they must have interaction, observation and conversation, from and with respectful educators (see chapter 4).

This part of article 29 relates directly to article 13, which asserts a child's right to freedom of expression, including 'freedom to seek, receive and impart information and ideas of all kinds regardless of frontiers, either orally, in writing or in print, in the form of art, or through any other media of the child's choice'. Iram Siraj-Blatchford and Kath Hirst (chapters 3 and 8) have discussed the importance of children being in a climate of learning where their home language and culture are valued and where respect for them is demonstrated. Wendy Scott (chapter 4) has drawn attention to the importance of creating for children a range of opportunities for creation and expression.

How does early educaré enable children to assert their right to express themselves, their love, their likes, their fears, their dislikes, their wants, their hates, their feelings? How often do adults try to make children smile, ask them for a kiss they do not want to give or limit their expression by either restricting their opportunities to 'speak' or to 'be' themselves?

Article 29b

the development of respect for human rights and fundamental freedoms, and for the principles enshrined in the charter of the United Nations.

> - How well do nurseries, schools, playgroups, creches, respect the rights of children?
> - What does a respectful service for children look like and feel like?
> - To what extent do educators foster respect for human rights, freedom of choice and principles of dignity, individualism and mutual respect enshrined in the charter?
> - Does the nursery teach children about their rights and enable them to discuss what having 'rights' means to them?
> - What does a respectful early childhood curriculum look like and feel like?
> - To what extent are children helped to understand that they have the right to make choices?

Jane was working with 3-year-old Allen and 4-month-old Naomi. Allen wanted Naomi to hold a set of plastic keys. Jane gently reminded Allen that Naomi was allowed to choose what she played with. She said, 'She can choose, she doesn't have to play with the one you like, you like to choose, she likes to choose as well.' Allen recognized this assertion and then gathered a small selection of toys and put them at the side of the baby: 'There – now she can choose.'

Young children learn lessons about human interaction from the youngest age. They need positive experiences and role models in their early years to help them to learn about being an individual, being different, special, unique and respecting one another, respecting differences, different ways, different personalities (see chapters 3 and 6). They need to know themselves in order to be able to cope with differences in conduct in group settings. Initiatives such as the *Fairness Project* (Griffiths and Davis, 1995) can help to develop work that fosters understanding of human rights, individualism and mutual respect.

How can people who work with babies have and show respect for human rights and principles of dignity? Establishing a key worker system (Rouse and Griffin; 1992; Goldschmied and Jackson, 1994; Whalley, 1994) where the same educator works with the same baby each day, feeds her, changes her, talks and plays with her is showing respect for her as a person, her dignity. Not just anyone can change her nappy, she has a right to dignity and respect for herself in the process, the right to be with someone who knows her, tunes into her minute but telling body language, remembers the experiences she enjoyed yesterday and offers them again today, sings special songs and rhymes at particular times, changing, playing, feeding, settling to sleep, and builds up a relationship with her parents so that they can know more about her day and the daytime educator can be told about her night-time and sleep patterns and other special pieces of information, making her educaré more holistic.

A respectful curriculum means children knowing what they are doing and why (see chapter 4).

Six 4-year-olds were sitting at a table colouring shapes. One of the group, Henry, was asked what he was doing. 'Colouring', he said. 'What are you colouring?' he was asked. 'Shapes,' said Henry. 'Oh! and what shape is this that you are colouring now?' was the next question. 'Don't know,' was Henry's reply, 'I'm just colouring it, like you have to.'

Comparing this observation with the work of the three boys of the same age in chapter 4 illustrates that the educator's sense of purpose and curriculum knowledge make the essential difference in curriculum decision-making.

A respectful curriculum means children being able to explore and experiment and make choices (see chapter 4).

A teacher of thirty-five children some aged 4, some just 5, in a reception classroom said: 'I want them to play more, but they don't have the space and I don't have the time.' Should such a classroom, with a teacher who knows what children need but is unable to provide it receive the confident mark?

Article 29c

The development of respect for the child's parents, his or her own cultural identity, language and values, for the national values of the country in which the child is living, the country from which he or she may originate, and for civilisations different from his or her own.

- How much respect is shown to parents?
- On what basis do educators work with parents?
- How are children encouraged to be proud of who they are, what they look like, how they speak, and to respect the differences of others?
- Does every bit of the provision look as if diversity of language, culture and identity is valued? Or does it look as if one culture and one language dominate?

Some young children will explore their fascination with things that are different without prejudice or inhibition. Simone (2 years and 6 months) and Jerome (1 year) were with their mothers at a table in a coffee shop and Alexis (10 months) was with her parents at a nearby table. Jerome was in his pushchair, Alexis was in a highchair being fed, Simone was wandering around holding her drinking cup. Simone was interested in the two babies. She watched as Jerome and Alexis struck up a 'conversation' and communicated together, following each other's gaze. Having watched for a while Simone got closer and focused on the babies, their faces and their hair. She looked closely into their eyes then purposefully moved towards Alexis and touched her head. She stroked her fine blonde hair several times then she moved to Jerome and stroked his tight, deep, black curls. She moved between the babies, touching their heads, feeling their hair. Was she feeling the differences she had noticed by looking? How were those differences made positive by the adults around her? Valuing differences, of appearance, skin tone and colour, hair colour and texture, language, culture, traditions, is something which can be nurtured from an early age (see chapter 3). We are aware now, that children as young as 3 (possibly younger) have already decided that one skin colour can be superior to another. 'Respect' must be nurtured: children are capable and quick learners, they will learn the messages we give them. Respectful educators will ensure that diversity and difference are celebrated and that children are empowered to 'be' themselves as well as learn beside others.

Article 29d

the preparation of the child for responsible life in a free society, in the spirit of understanding, peace, tolerance, equality of sexes, and friendship among all peoples, ethnic, national and religious groups and persons of indigenous origin.

- Is there a climate of co-operation, equality of opportunity?
- Are the teaching and care practices those that value all children equally and enable them to make choices for themselves?
- Do staff value children's rights to challenge, question and assert themselves?
- Are children taught how they might assert themselves without aggression?

For a 3-year-old, principles of mutual respect, self-assertion and peace may mean enabling her to assert her anger when another child hits her. I have heard children tell nursery workers 'He hit me' and the reply comes: 'We don't hit each other here.' What does this do? It immediately denies the child any assertion and fails to deal with the transgression. An alternative strategy is not to use adult power alone to intervene when 3-year-olds hit each other, but to give children strategies to resolve those conflicts. With support, young children can begin to assert themselves (Whalley, 1994). They can learn to say 'no' in an assertive voice – and they can shout, 'Don't do that to me.' They often need help to decide what to say. It is not enough for an educator to tell a child, 'Tell her not to do that' – children who are learning about language need help with the words and strategies, they may need the adult to say a phrase that they can then repeat. It often takes time to help children decide what they want to say and to provide encouragement as they speak to the child who has hurt or offended them. In time, such an approach can empower children to assert their rights and protect themselves (Nutbrown, 1994b). This way of working is not about judgements, or rights and wrongs as seen through the eyes of the educator. It is about self-assertion, children protecting themselves, their feelings and their bodies. It is about children developing skills for living which – in the words of the UN Convention – 'foster respect, human rights, freedom of choice, and principles of dignity, individualism and mutual respect'.

Ahmed, aged 4 years and 2 months, was playing outside in the nursery garden when a child hit him and took away the bike he was riding. He took another bike, cornered the offender and said, repeatedly, 'You hit me, that was wrong, say sorry.' He repeated these words until he extracted the apology he needed and then rode off on his bike, satisfied that justice had been done. The development of understanding, peace and tolerance can begin with encouraging children to assert themselves in such ways and finding appropriate ways to support the offenders too, ensuring that their dignity is protected and that they have an opportunity to learn from their experiences.

Article 29e

the development of respect for the natural environment.

- How do the outdoor experiences offered to children in nurseries, schools, playgroups, creches, foster an appreciation, understanding and respect for the natural environment?
- Are children able to explore the feeling of wet grass under their feet, lie beneath a cloudy sky on a summer day, crawl through some undergrowth or a mossy tunnel?
- Is there a policy of recycling, care for the outdoors, for wildlife, and an understanding about the elements?
- Are children encouraged to think about pollution, energy conservation and protection of their world in ways that they can understand?

In many settings children dig in the garden, plant seeds, water plants, feed the birds in wintertime, watch insects – spiders, wood lice, ladybirds and butterflies – crawling on the ground or flying, or hiding among the foliage.

If children have played with the natural components of the world they are in a better position to develop further concepts through these media. Children with few encounters with these natural materials will need time to explore their properties and attributes before they can progress to deeper learning constructs. Wendy Scott and Tricia David (chapters 4 and 9) have described how educators might enable these capabilities to be developed.

The restrictions which are placed on children and the consequences of these in terms of their subsequent development were considered by Tinbergen (1976), who discussed the ways in which young children learn through play in their natural environments. Tinbergen suggested that society has inhibited children's freedom to play and, just as young animals find their own way of learning, young children could do the same if they were in an appropriate environment. A recent study conducted by Barnardo's illuminated parents' fears of their children playing outdoors unsupervised – another instance of children's freedom to play being further curtailed in order to keep them safe.

Children's best interests would be served if provision for the youngest children in our world were to be examined to see how well it respects the rights of children and enables them to experience the quality of education and care which is enshrined in article 29, and other articles in the Convention. The Convention asserts children's rights to education, yet two recent studies (Shelter, 1995; Education for Sick Children, 1995) highlight that children who are homeless and ill often miss out on this fundamental right. More flexible and better resourced systems are needed to realize the rights of more vulnerable children to education.

Early education and affective development

We know much more about the cognitive development of babies. Recently we have recognized, in an academic sense, the fact that the youngest babies have an awesome capacity to make sense of their world, to explore, examine and understand it (Trevarthen, 1992).

Until recent years it was traditional for nursery education in Britain to focus on children's early social and emotional development and the development of talk (once called language development). More recently – in less than the last ten years – it has been more fully acknowledged that nursery education, and latterly other forms of early childhood provision, has a part to play in other aspects of children's development, their cognitive growth, too. Some 3- and 4-year-old children can write their names and other things, many have begun to read, most know a lot about mathematical and scientific phenomena – all tackle technology, at home and in group education settings, in a way that puts many adults to shame. Some nursery schools have pioneered the use of computers by young children. Brailsford (1994) has published her work on the use of computers to support many aspects of the curriculum and this is now in the hands of early years educators nationwide. Great strides have been made in different areas of learning and experience. While early years educators continue to break new ground in terms of early years practice and continue to stress the cognitive benefits of early education to those who value it most, they must also continue in the best traditions of nursery education to nurture children's being, their inner selves, promote positive feelings of self-worth, competence and belief, and break new ground in the fostering of the development of the emotions too.

For we now know that there are real links between children's emotional and cognitive patterns. Research is in its infancy but Athey's work on schemas (1990) and Goldschmied's work on children under 3 (Goldschmied and Jackson, 1994) have triggered interest in the need to foster security and positive self-identity and opened our eyes to a clearer picture of what can be meant by a holistic approach.

Gerison Lansdown indicated in chapter 1 that it took ten years to draft the United Nations Convention on the Rights of the Child. How long will it take to realize the rights that are now enshrined in international law? Over fifty years ago Korzack so respected the children in his care that he voluntarily accompanied them to torture and death in the gas chambers. No such ultimate sacrifice in the interests of children is required of early childhood educators in the UK today, but the UN Convention does call upon them to work towards the realization of children's rights, and that means giving something of themselves.

There are obligations on governments, yes, but there are responsibilities for every adult citizen too. The first UK report on progress in implementing the UN Convention was delivered in 1994, the next is due in 1999. What new era will the next millennium bring for children?

Now is the time that everyone with an interest in children must be clear about who they are and their own identity, so that they can work with others to pursue common goals.

Now is the time for every adult to stand up for the rights of children, to work toward the acceptance of children as respected members of the community and recognized capable learners. Can we afford not to?

Endword

Children's rights and international protection

Each new generation offers humanity another chance.

If we ensure the survival and development of children in all parts of the world, protect them from harm and exploitation and enable them to participate in decisions directly affecting their lives, we will surely build the foundation of the just society we all want and that children deserve.

UNICEF

References

Ainscow, M. (1995) Education for all: making it happen. Keynote address presented at the International Special Education Congress, Birmingham, England, April 1995.

Athey, C. (1990) *Extending Thought in Young Children – A Parent-Teacher Partnership,*. Paul Chapman, London.

Audit Commission Directorate of Local Government Studies (1994) *Audit Commission Study of Under Fives Education: Field Visits – Outline of Purposes,* Audit Commission, London.

Bailey, D. and Hall, S. (eds.) (1992) *Critical Decade: Black British Photography in the 80s,* Ten-8, Vol. 2, no. 3.

Bailey, R. (forthcoming) *Play and Problem Solving.* Work in progress, Christ Church College, Canterbury.

Ball C. (1994) *Start Right,* RSA, London

Barrett, G. (1986) *Starting School: an Evaluation of the Experience,* AMMA, London.

Barrs, M., Ellis, S., Hester, H. and Thomas, A. (1991) *Patterns of Learning – The Primary Language Record and the National Curriculum,* Centre for Language in Primary Education, London.

Bartholemew, L. and Bruce, T. (1993) *Getting to Know You – A Guide to Record-Keeping in Early Childhood Education and Care,* Hodder and Stoughton, London.

Bastiani, J. (1989) *Working with Parents: A Whole School Approach,* Routledge, London.

Bennett, N. and Kell, J. (1989) *A Good Start?,* Blackwell, Oxford.

Berlyne, D. E. (1970) Children's reasoning and thinking, in P. H. Mussen (ed.) *Carmichael's Manual of Child Psychology,* 3rd edn, Wiley, New York.

Bernstein, B. (1992) *The Structuring of Pedagogic Discourse.* Vol. IV: *Class, Codes and Control,* Routledge, London.

Biggs, A. and Edwards, A. (1992) 'I treat them all the same' – teacher-pupil talk in multi-ethnic classrooms, *Language and Education,* Vol. 5, no. 3, pp. 161–76.

Bird, G. and Buckley, S. (1994) *Meeting the Educational Needs of Children with Down's Syndrome. A Handbook for Teachers,* University of Portsmouth, England.

Bradshaw, J. (1990) *Child Poverty and Deprivation in the UK,* National Children's Bureau, London.

Brailsford, M. (1994) *Using Computers in the Nursery,* OMEP (UK), London.

Braun, D. (1992) Working with parents, in G. Pugh (ed.) op. cit.

Bredekamp, S. (ed.) (1987) *Developmentally Appropriate Practice in Early Childhood Programs Serving Children from Birth Through Age Eight*, NAEYC, Washington.

Brierley, J. (1980) *Children's Well-Being – Growth, Development and Learning from Conception to Adolescence*, NFER, Slough.

Brierley, J. (1987) *Give Me a Child Until He Is Seven*, Falmer Press, Lewes.

Bruce, T. (1987) *Early Childhood Education*, Hodder and Stoughton, London.

Bruner, J. (1977) *The Process of Instructions*, Harvard University Press, Cambridge, Mass.

Bruner, J., Jolly, S. and Sylva, K. (1976) *Play and Its Role in the Development of the Child*, Penguin, London.

Bruner, J. (1990) *Acts of Meaning*, Harvard University Press, Cambridge, Mass.

Buckley, S. (1994) Early intervention, the state of the art, in B. Carpenter (ed.) *Early Intervention, Where Are We Now?*, Westminster College, Oxford.

Burns. A. (1985) *Home and School: A Child's Eye View*, Allen and Unwin, London.

Carpenter, B. (1995) Building an inclusive curriculum, in K. Ashcroft and D. Palacio (eds.) *A Primary Teacher's Guide to the New National Curriculum*, Falmer Press, London.

Carpenter, B. and Herbert, E. (1994) School based support, in P. Mittler and H. Mittler (eds.) *Innovations in Family Support for People with Learning Difficulties* Lisieux Hall, Chorley.

Central Statistical Office (1995) *Social Trends 25*, HMSO, London.

Centre for Human Rights (1991) *General Guidelines Regarding the Form and Content of Initial Reports to be Submitted by States Parties under Article 44,1(a) of the UN Convention on the Rights of the Child*, Centre for Human Rights, Geneva, October.

Children's Rights Development Unit (1994) *UK Agenda for Children*, Children's Rights Development Unit, London.

Children's Rights Office (1995) *Building Small Democracies: The Implications of the UN Convention on the Rights of the Child for Respecting Children's Civil Rights in the Family*, Children's Rights Office, London.

Clark, C., Dyson, A. and Millward, A. (eds.) (1995) *Towards Inclusive Schooling*, David Fulton, London.

Commission on Social Justice/Institute for Public Policy Research (1994) *Social Justice – Strategies for National Renewal*, Vintage, London.

Committee on the Rights of the Child (1995) *Consideration of reports of State Parties: United Kingdom of Great Britain and Northern Ireland*, CRC/C/SR.205, January.

Cousins, J. (1990) 'Are your little Humpty Dumpties sinking or floating?' What sense do children of four make of the reception class at school? Different conceptions at the time of transition, *Early Years*, Vol. 10, no. 2, pp. 28–31.

Cross, W. (1985) Black identity: rediscovering the distinctions between personal identity and reference group orientation, in M. Spencer, *et al.* (eds.) *Beginnings: The Social and Affective Development of Black Children*, N. J. Erlbaum, Hillsdale.

Cummins, J. (1984) *Bilingualism and Special Education: Issues in Assessment and Pedagogy*, Multilingual Matters, 6.

Cunningham, C. (1994) Telling parents their child has a disability, in P. Mittler and H. Mittler (eds.) *Innovations in Family Support for People with Learning Difficulties*, Lisieux Hall, Chorley.

Curtis A. (1994) *Training to Work with Young Children in Europe*, OMEP, London.

Dahlberg, G. (1991) *Empathy and social control: on parent-child relationships in the context of modern childhood.* Paper presented at the ISSBD Conference, Minneapolis, USA.

David, T. (1990) *Under Five – Under Educated?*, Open University Press, Milton Keynes.

David, T. (1992a) Curriculum in the early years, in G. Pugh (ed.) op. cit.

David, T. (1992b) *What do parents in Britain and Belgium want their children to learn in nursery?* Paper presented at the XXth World Congress of OMEP, University of Northern Arizona, August 1992.

David, T. (1993) Educating children under five in the UK, in T. David (ed.) *Educational Provision for our Youngest Children: European Perspectives*, Paul Chapman, London.

David, T., Curtis, A. and Siraj-Blatchford, I. (1993) *Effective Teaching in the Early Years: Fostering Children's Learning in Nursery and Infant Classes*, OMEP, London.

David, T. and Nutbrown, C. (eds.) (1993) *The Universal and the National in Preschool Provision*, UNESCO, Paris.

Davies, B. (1989) *Frogs and Snails and Feminist Tales*, Allen and Unwin, St Leonards, NSW.

Dearing, R. (1994) *The National Curriculum and its Assessment: Final Report*, SCAA, London.

Deloache, J. S. and Brown, A. L. (1987) The early emergence of planning skills in children, in J. Bruner and H. Haste (eds.) *Making Sense*, Methuen, London.

DEMOS (1995) *The Time Squeeze*, DEMOS, London.

Department for Education (1993) *Statutory Instrument 1981/909* Circular 14/93, HMSO, London.

Department for Education (1994) *The Code of Practice for the Identification and Assessment of Special Educational Needs*, HMSO, London.

Department for Education and Employment/Department of Health (1995) *Quality Assurance Regime for Institutions which redeem vouchers for preschool education*, DFEE, London.

Department for Education and Employment (1996) *Nursery Education scheme: the next steps*, DFEE, London.

Department of Education and Science (1967) *Children and the Primary Schools: A Report of the Central Advisory Council for Education (England)*, Vol. 1, HMSO, London.

Department of Education and Science (1978) *Report of the Committee of Enquiry into the Education of Handicapped Children and Young People* (Warnock Report), HMSO, London.

Department of Education and Science (1985) *Education for All*, (Swann Report), HMSO, London.

Department of Education and Science (1989) *Aspects of Primary Education: The Education of Children Under Five*, HMSO, London.

Department of Education and Science (1990) *Starting with Quality: Report of the Committee of Inquiry into the Educational Experiences Offered to 3 and 4 Year Olds*, HMSO, London.

Department of Health (1989) *The Children Act*, HMSO, London.

Dessent, T. (1987) *Making the Ordinary School Special*, Falmer Press, Lewes.

Donaldson, M. (1978) *Children's Minds*, Fontana, Glasgow.

Drummond, M. J. (1993) *Assessing Children's Learning*, David Fulton, London.

Drummond, M. J. (1995) What are four year olds like? Setting the scene, in T. David and C. Nutbrown (eds.) *Four-Year-Olds in School: Learning Properly?*, OMEP (UK), London.

Drummond, M. J. and Nutbrown C. (1992) Observing and assessing young children, in G. Pugh (ed.) op. cit.

Drummond, M. J., Rouse, D. and Pugh, G. (1992) *Making Assessment Work*, NCB/NES Arnold, London.

Durkheim, E. (1922) Education and Society, in A. Giddens, (1972) *Emile Durkheim: Selected Writings*, Cambridge University Press.

Dweck, C. and Leggett (1988) A social cognitive approach to motivation and personality, *Psychological Review* Vol.. 95, no. 2, pp. 256–73.

Early Years Curriculum Group (1989) *The Early Years Curriculum and the National Curriculum*, Trentham Books, Stoke-on-Trent.

Education for Sick Children (1995) *Directory of Current Provision in England and Wales*, National Association for Education for Sick Children, London.

Ferguson, D. and Meyer, G. (1991) *Ecological Assessment*, University of Oregon (Schools Project).

Fisher, J. (1995) Planning a curriculum for the early years classroom, *Early Education*, British Association for Early Childhood Education, London.

Fisher, J. (in press) *Starting from the Child*, Open University Press, Milton Keynes.

Fitzpatrick, F. (1987) *The Open Door*, Multilingual Matters,

Gay, G. (1985) Implications of selected models of ethnic identity development for educators, *Journal of Negro Education*, Vol. 54, no. 1.

Gillborn, D. (1990) *'Race', Ethnicity and Education*, Unwin Hyman, London.

Giroux, H. and McLaren, P. (eds.) (1994) *Between Borders: Pedagogy and the Politics of Cultural Studies*, Routledge, London.

Goldschmied, E. and Jackson, S. (1994) *People Under Three*, Routledge, London.

Griffiths, M. and Davis, C. (1995) *In Fairness to Children*, David Fulton, London.

Grossberg, L. (1994) Introduction: bringing it all back home – pedagogy and cultural studies, in H. Giroux and P. McLaren (eds.) op. cit.

Grugeon, E. and Woods, P. (1990) *Educating All: Multicultural Perspectives in the Primary School*, Routledge, London

Gura, P. (ed.) (1992) *Exploring Learning – Young Children and Block-Play*, Paul Chapman, London.

Hall, S. (1992) Race, culture and communications: looking backward and forward in cultural studies, *Rethinking Marxism*, Vol. 5, pp. 10–18.

Hallden, G. (1991) The child as project and child as being: parents' ideas as frames of reference, *Children and Society*, Vol. 5, no. 4, pp. 334–46.

Hampshire Education Authority (1995) Hampshire early years pack, IASS, Hampshire Education Authority.

Handy, C. (1994) *The Empty Raincoat*, Hutchinson, London.

Hannon, P. (1995) *Literacy, Home and School; Research and Practice in Teaching Literacy with Parents*, Falmer Press, London.

Hannon, P., Weinberger, J. and Nutbrown, C. (1991). A study of ways of working with parents to promote early literacy development, *Research Papers in Education*, Vol. 6, no. 2, pp. 77–97.

Hart, M. (1994) in *Our Present is Their Future*, BAECE video transcript.

Hazareesingh, S., Simms, K. and Andeson, P. (1989) *Educating the Whole Child – A Holistic Approach to Education in the Early Years,* Building Blocks Early Years Project/Save the Children, Equality Learning Centre, 357 Holloway Road, London N7 6PA.

Herbert, E. (1994) Becoming a special family, in T. David (ed.) *Working Together for Young Children,* Routledge, London.

Herbert, E. and Carpenter, B. (1994) Fathers – the secondary partners: professional perceptions and a father's reflections, *Children and Society,* Vol. 8, no. 1, pp. 31–41.

Her Majesty's Government (1992) *Education (Schools) Act,* HMSO, London.

Hill, E. (1980) *Where's Spot?,* Heinemann, London.

Hillman, M., Adams, J. and Whitelegg, J. (1990) *One False Move . . . A Study of Children's Independent Mobility,* Policy Studies Institute, London.

Hirst, K. and Hannon, P. (1990) An evaluation of a preschool home teaching project, *Educational Research,* Vol. 32, no. 1, pp. 33–9.

HMI (1989) *The Education of Children Under Five,* HMSO, London.

HMSO (1988) *Education Reform Act,* HMSO, London.

HMSO (1988) *Occupational Mortality in England and Wales – Childhood Supplement OPCS,* HMSO, London.

HMSO (1993) *The Education Act,* part 3, HMSO, London.

HMSO (1994) *The UK's First Report to the UN Committee on the Rights of the Child,* HMSO, London.

Hornby, G. (1995) *Working with Parents of Children with Special Educational Needs,* Cassell, London.

House of Commons Select Committee for Education, Science and Arts (1989) *Educational Provision for the Under Fives,* HMSO, London.

House of Commons Select Committee for Education, Science and Arts (1994) *Educational Provision for the Under Fives,* HMSO, London

Humphreys, S., Mack, J. and Perks, R. (1988) *A Century of Childhood,* Sidgwick and Jackson, London.

Hurst, V. (1991) *Planning for Early Learning and Education in the First Five Years,* Paul Chapman, London.

Hutt, S. J., Tyler, S., Hutt, C. and Christopherson, H. (1989) *Play, Exploration and Learning,* Routledge, London.

Isaacs, S. (1929) *The Nursery Years,* Routledge & Kegan Paul, London.

Ishigaki, E. (1995) How have the 'Rights of the Child' been taught in kindergarten

Jowett, S. and Baginsky, M. with MacNeil, M. M., (1991) *Building bridges: Parental Involvement in Schools,* NFER/Nelson, Windsor.

Jowett, S. and Sylva, K. (1986) Does kind of pre-school matter?, *Educational Research,* Vol. 28, no. 1, pp. 21–31.

Jupp, S. (1992) *Making the Right Start : A Practical Guide to Help Break the News to Families when their Baby has been Born with a Disability,* Open Eyed Publication, Hyde, Cheshire.

Kakar, S. (1981) *The Inner World. A Psycho-analytic Study of Childhood and Society in India,* Oxford University Press, New Delhi.

Katz, L. and Chard, S. (1989) *Engaging Children's Minds: The Project Approach,* Ablex Publishing Corporation, New Jersey.

Katz, L. and McLellan, D. (1991) *The Teacher's Role in the Social Development of Young Children,* ERIC Clearing House on Elementary and Early Childhood

Education, Urbana, I.L., USA.

King, R. (1978) *All Things Bright and Beautiful?*, Wiley, Chichester.

Kumar, V. and National Children's Bureau (1993) *Poverty and Inequality in the UK: The Effects on Children*, National Children's Bureau, London.

Lally, M. (1991) *The Nursery Teacher in Action*, Paul Chapman, London.

Lang, P. (1995) The place of PSE in the primary school, in J. and I. Siraj-Blatchford (eds.) op. cit.

Lansdown, G. and Newell, P. (eds.) (1994) *UK Agenda for Children*, London, Children's Rights Development Unit, London.

Lawrence, D. (1988) *Enhancing Self-Esteem in the Classroom*, Paul Chapman, London.

Leon, D. (1991) Influence of birthweight on differences in infant mortality by social class and legitimacy, *British Medical Journals* no. 303, pp 964–7.

Lewis, A. (1991) *Primary Special Needs and the National Curriculum*, Routledge, London.

Lewis, A (1995) *Children's Understanding about Disability*, London: Routledge.

Lloyd, B. (1987) Social representations of gender, in J. Bruner, and H. Haste (eds.) *Making Sense: The Child's Construction of the World*, Routledge, London.

Lloyd, B. and Duveen, G. (1992) *Gender Identities and Education*, Harvester Wheatsheaf, Hemel Hempstead.

Lubeck, S. (1986) *Sandbox Society*, Falmer, Lewes.

Mac an Ghaill, M. (1992) Coming of age in 1980s England: reconceptualising black students' experience, in D. Gill, B. Mayor and M. Blair (eds.) *Racism and Education: Structures and Strategies*, Sage in association with Open University Press, London.

Mahony, P. (1985) *Schools for the Boys*, Hutchinson, London.

Malaguzzi, L. (1992) *A Charter of Rights*, Municipality of Reggio Emilia, Italy.

Matthews, J. (1995) *Helping Children to Draw and Paint in Early Childhood*, Hodder and Stoughton, London.

Maximé, J. E. (1991) *Towards a Transcultural Approach with Under-Sevens*, Report of the Early Years Trainers Anti-Racist Network, London.

Mayall, B. (ed.) (1994) *Children's Childhoods Observed and Experienced*, Falmer Press, London.

Miller, S. (1973) Ends, means and galumphing: some leitmotifs of play, *American Anthropologist*, Vol. 75, pp. 87–98.

Ministry of Education (1993) *Te Whariki – Draft Guidelines for Developmentally Appropriate Programmes in Early Childhood Services*, Learning Media Ltd, Box 3293, Wellington, NZ.

Mittler, P. and Mittler, H. (1994) A framework for support, in P. Mittler and H. Mittler (eds.) *Innovations in Family Support for People with Learning Difficulties*, Lisieux Hall, Chorley.

Moyles, J. (1989) *Just Playing?*, Open University Press, Buckingham.

National Commission on Education (1994) *Learning to Succeed*, Report of the National Commission on Education, Paul Hamlyn, London.

National Occupational Standards for Working with Young Children and their Families (1994) 2nd edn, HMSO, London.

Newell, P. (1991) *The UN Convention and Children's Rights in the UK*, National Children's Bureau, London.

Newham Education Authority (1995) *Foundations for Our Future*, Newham Council.

Nutbrown, C. (1994a) *Threads of Thinking: Young Children Learning and the Role of Early Education*, Paul Chapman, London.

Nutbrown, C. (1994b) Young children in educational establishments, in T. David (ed.) *Working Together for Young Children*, Routledge, London.

OFSTED (1993) *The Handbook for the Inspection of Schools*, HMSO, London.

OFSTED (1994) *First Class*, HMSO, London.

Ogilvy, B., Cheyne, J. and Schafer, R. (1991) Staff attitudes and perception in multicultural nursery schools, *Early Child Development and Care*, Vol. 64.

Oldman, D. (1994) Childhood as a mode of Production, in Mayall, B. op. cit.

OPCS, (1989) *Occupational Mortality England and Wales – Childhood Supplement*, HMSO, London.

Oxfordshire County Council (1991) *Quality in Learning for Under Fives*, Oxfordshire County Council.

Paley, V. G. (1984) *Boys and Girls: Superheroes in the Doll Corner*, Chicago University Press.

Paley, V. G. (1986) *Mollie is Three*, Chicago University Press.

Paley, V. G. (1988) *Bad Guys Don't Have Birthdays*, Chicago University Press.

Paley, V. G. (1990) *The Boy Who Would be a Helicopter*, Chicago University Press.

Pinsent, P. (1992) *Language, Culture and Young Children*, David Fulton, London.

Pugh, G. (ed.) (1992) *Contemporary Issues in the Early Years: Working Collaboratively for Children*, NCB/PCP, London.

Pugh, G. and De'Ath, E. (1989) *Towards Partnership in the Early Years*, National Children's Bureau, London.

Pugh, G., De'Ath, E. and Smith, C. (1992) *Confident Parents, Confident Children: Policy and Practice in Parent Education and Support*, National Children's Bureau, London.

Preschool Playgroups Association (1991) *What Children Learn in Playgroup – A PPA Curriculum*, PPA, London.

Purkey, W. (1970) *Self-concept and School Achievement*, Paul Chapman, London.

Reggio Children (1995) *A Journey Into the Rights of Children*, Municipality of Reggio Emilia, Italy.

Roberts, R. (1995) *Self-esteem and Successful Early Learning*, Hodder and Stoughton, London.

Rodd, J., (1994) *Leadership in the Early Years*, Open University Press, Buckingham.

Rosen, M. (ed.) (1994) *The Penguin Book of Childhood*, Penguin, London.

Rouse, D., and Griffin, S. (1992) *Quality for the Under Threes*, in G. Pugh (ed.) op. cit.

Rousseau, J.-J. (1762) *Émile* (published in translation in 1911), Dent, London.

Runnymede Trust (1993) *Equality Assurance in Schools; Quality, Identity, Society*, Trentham Books, Stoke-on-Trent.

Saracho, O. (1992) The future of teacher education in a changing world, *Early Child Development and Care*, Vol. 78, pp. 225–9.

School Curriculum and Assessment Authority (SCAA) (1995) *Pre-school Education Consultation – Desirable Outcomes for Children's Learning and Guidance for Providers – Draft Proposals*. SCAA and Central Office of Information, London.

School Curriculum and Assessment Authority (SCAA) (1996) *Nursery Education – desirable outcomes for children's learning on entering compulsory education*, SCAA and DFEE, London.

Sharp, C. (1995) *School Entry and the Impact of Season of Birth on Attainment*, NFER Research Summary, London, September.

Sharp, C., Hutchison, D. and Whetton C. (1994) *How do Season of Birth and Length of Schooling Affect Children's Attainment at Key Stage 1?*, NEFR, London.

Sharp, R. and Green, A. (1975) *Education and Social Control*, Routledge and Kegan Paul, London.

Shelter (1995) *No Place to Learn: Homeless Children and Education*, Shelter, London.

Siraj-Blatchford, I. (1992) Why understanding cultural differences is not enough, in G. Pugh, (ed.) op. cit.

Siraj-Blatchford, I. (1994) *The Early Years: Laying the Foundations for Racial Equality*, Trentham Books, Stoke-on-Trent.

Siraj-Blatchford, J. and Siraj-Blatchford, I. (eds.) (1995) *Educating the Whole Child: Cross-Curricular Skills, Themes and Dimensions*, Open University Press, Buckingham.

Smail, D. (1984) *Taking Care: An Alternative to Therapy*, Dent, London.

Smith, E. and Bennett, N. (1995) Play away, *Child Education*, Vol. 73, no. 3, pp. 64–5.

Smith, F. (1982) *Understanding Reading*, Holt, Rinehart and Winston, London.

Stone, M. (1981) *The Education of the Black Child in Britain: The Myth of Multiracial Education*, Fontana, London.

Sutton-Smith, B. (ed.) (1979) *Play and Learning*, Gardner Press, New York.

Sylva, K. (1994) A curriculum for early learning. Appendix C in C. Ball, op. cit.

Sylva, K., Roy, C. and Painter, M. (1980) *Childwatching at Playgroup and Nursery School*, Grant McIntyre, London.

Thompson, F. (1945) *Larkrise to Candleford*, Oxford University Press.

Tinbergen, N. (1976) *The Importance of Being Playful*, British Association for Early Childhood Education, London.

Tizard, B. and Hughes, M. (1984) *Young Children Learning*, Fontana, London.

Torkington, K. (1986) Involving parents in the primary curriculum, in M. Hughes (ed.) *Involving Parents in the Primary Curriculum*, Exeter University Occasional Paper, Perspectives no. 24, Exeter.

Trevarthen, C. (1992a) An infant's motives for speaking and thinking in the culture, in A. H. Wold (ed.) *The Dialogical Alternative*, Oxford University Press.

Trevarthen, C. (1992b) in *Play for Tomorrow*, documentary shown on BBC2.

UN (1989) *Convention on the Rights of the Child*, United Nations, New York.

Verhallen, M., Appel, R. and Schoonen, R. (1989) Language functions in early childhood education: the cognitive–linguistic experiences of bilingual and monolingual children, *Language and Education*, Vol. 3, no. 2, pp. 109–30.

Villen, K. (1993) Pre-School education in Denmark, in T. David (ed.) *Educational Provision for our Youngest Children: European Perspectives*, Paul Chapman, London.

Vygotsky, L. S. (1962) *Thought and Language*, MIT Press, Cambridge, Mass.

Vygotsky, L. S. (1978) *Mind in Society: The Development of Higher Level Psychological Processes*, Harvard University Press, Cambridge, Mass.

Walkerdine, V. (1987) Sex, power and pedagogy, in M. Arnot and G. Weiner (eds.) *Gender and the Politics of Schooling*, Unwin Hyman, London.

Walton, Lord (1995) *Briefing Paper 1*, National Commission on Education, London.

Weinberger, J., Hannon, P. and Nutbrown, C. (1990) *Ways of Working with Parents to Promote Early Literacy Development*. USDE Papers in Education no. 14, University of Sheffield Division of Education.

Wells, G. (1987) *The Meaning Makers: Children Learning Language and Using*

Language to Learn, Hodder and Stoughton, London.

Westminster Education Authority (1992) *Great Expectations*, Westminster LEA, London.

Whalley, M. (1992) Working as a team, in G. Pugh (ed.) op. cit.

Whalley, M. (1994) *Learning to be Strong*, Hodder and Stoughton, London.

Williams, V. (1991) *Boxed In*, Red Fox, London.

Willis, P. (1977) *Learning to Labour*, Saxon House, London.

Wolfendale, S. (1989) *Parental Involvement: Developing Networks between School, Home, Community*, Cassell, London.

Wolfendale, S. (1990) *All about Me*, NES Arnold, London.

Wolfendale, S. (1993) *Baseline Assessment: A Review of Current Practice, Issues and Strategies for Effective Implementation*, OMEP, London and Trentham Books, Stoke-on-Trent.

Wolfendale, S. and Wooster, J. (1992) Meeting special needs in the early years, in G. Pugh (ed.) op. cit.

Wood, D. (1988) *How Young Children Think and Learn*, Blackwell, Oxford.

Woodrofe, C. (1993) *Teenagers and Health – The Key Data*, Open University Press, Buckingham.

Wright, C. (1992) Early Education: multiracial primary school classrooms, in D. Gill, B. Mayor and M. Blair (eds.) *Racism and Education: Structures and Strategies*, Sage in association with Open University, London.

Author Index

Adams, 91
Ainscow, 60
Appel, 30
Athey, 42, 45, 85, 107
Audit Commission, 100

Baginsky, 67
Bailey, 26
Bailey, 95
Ball, 35, 71
Barrett, 37
Barrs, 52
Bartholomew , 52
Bastiani, 59
Bennett, 91, 94
Berleyne, 94
Bernstein, 24
Biggs, 29
Bird, 58
Bradshaw, 84
Brailsford, 107
Braun, 82
Bredekamp, 40
Brierley, 42, 47
Brown, 92
Bruce, 40, 52
Bruner, 41, 92
Buckley, 57, 58
Burns, 65

Carpenter, 58, 62, 66
Centre for Human Rights, 2
Chard, 36, 41
Cheyne, 29
Children's Rights Development
    Unit, 101
Children's Rights Office, 10
Clark, 61
Commission on Social Justice,
    51

Committee on the Rights of the
    Child, 3
Cousins, 36
Cross, 25
Cummins, 30
Cunningham, 58
Curtis, 36, 71

Dahlberg, 91
David, 36, 62, 65, 82, 91
Davies, 24, 103
De'Ath, 64, 89, 100
Dearing, 72
Delaroche, 92
DEMOS, 97
Department for Education, 1, 77
Department for Education and
    Employment, 11, 100
Department of education and
    science, 24
DES, 25, 26, 33, 34, 35, 38, 65,
    75, 91, 95
Dessent, 59
DOH, 100
Donaldson, 36, 42, 45, 49, 50,
    51, 53, 92
Drummond, 61, 91
Durkenheim, xv
Duveen, 24
Dweck, 43
Dyson, 61

Early Years Curriculum Group, 35
Education for Sick Children, 106
Edwards, 29

Ferguson, 57
Fisher, 41
Fitzpatrick, 30

Gay, 25
Gillborn, 26
Goldschmied, 103, 107
Green, 96
Griffin, 57, 103
Griffiths, 103
Grossberg, 26
Gura, 36, 54

Hall, 26
Hallden, 91
Hampshire LEA, 38
Handy, 97
Hannon, 49, 85, 86, 87
Hart, 41
Hazaraeesingh, xiii
House of Commons Select
   Committee, 34
Hepworth, 55
Herbert, 57, 58, 66
Hill, E., 46
Hillman, 91
Hirst, 85, 87
HMSO, 2, 5, 66
Hornby, 63
Hughes, 36, 96
Humphreys, 90
Hurst, 42
Hutchinson, 37
Hutt, 94

Isaacs, 92
Ishigaki, 72

Jackson, 103, 107
Jolly, 41
Jowett, 37, 67
Jupp, 58

Kakar, xiv
Katz, 36, 38, 41
Kell, 91
King, 96
Kumar, 5

Lally, 41
Lang, 25
Lansdown, 2, 9
Lawrence, 24
Lewis, 60, 61, 62
Lloyd, 24, 27, 28
Lubeck, 96

Mac an Ghaill, 26
Mack, 90
MacNeil, 67
Mahony, 26
Malaguzzi, 39, 43
Matthews, 36
Maximé, 25
Mayell, xv
McLellan, 38
Meyer, 57
Miller, 94
Millward, 61
Ministry of Education (New Zealand),
   39
Mittler, H. 63
Mittler, P. 63
Moyles, 94

National Commission on Education
   (1993), 35
National Commission on Education
   (1994), 69
Newell, 2, 9, 81
Newell, 84, 101
Newham LEA, 38
Nutbrown, 42, 45, 49, 50, 52, 53,
   64, 85, 91

OFSTED, 13, 15, 18, 20, 91
Ogilvy, 29
Oldman, xv
OPCS, 5
Oxfordshire County Council, 53

Painter, 94
Paley, 37
Perks, 90
Pinsent, 30
PPA, 42, 45, 51
Pugh, 64, 89, 100
Purkey, 24

Reggio Children, 39, 41
Roberts, 38
Rodd, 66
Rosen, 51
Rouse, 42, 45, 51, 57, 103
Roy, 94
Runnymead Trust, 25

Saracho, 69
SCAA, 40, 55, 82, 83, 86, 100

Schaffer, 29
School Curriculum and Assessment
   Authority, xvii
Schoonen, 30
SCOPE, 58
Sharp, 37, 96
Shelter, 106
Siraj-Blatchford, I., 24, 25, 27,
   36, 59, 85
Siraj-Blatchford, J. 24, 27
Smith, 89, 100
Smith, 94
Stone, 27
Sutton-Smith, 96
Sylva, 37, 41, 43, 71, 94

Thompson, 90
Tinbergen, 106
Tizard, 36, 96
Torkington, 82
Trevarthen, 38, 92, 107

UN, 90
United Nations, 23

Verhallen, 30
Villen, xiv
Vygotsky, 36, 41, 46, 92

Walkerdine, 28
Walton, 69
Weinberger, 49
Wells, 36
Westminster LEA 38
Whalley, 52, 63, 88, 103
Whetton, 37
Whitelegg, 91
Williams, 46
Willis, 26
Wolfendale, 50, 52, 57, 59, 64
Wood, 36
Wooster, 59
Wright, 28

Index

abuse, 6, 84
achievement, 11, 24, 52, 59, 69
adult behaviour, 24
adult knowledge, 45, 54
adult power, 105
adult's responsibility, 41
advocates for children, 80
affective dimension of learning, 38
anti racist, sexist, classist practice, 32
anti-discriminatory activities and
    practice, 32, 33
apprenticeship approach, 36
Article 2, 23, 70, 82, 89
Article 3, 4, 8, 43, 70
Article 4, 3
Article 5, 7
Article 6, 56
Article 12, 5, 7, 8, 35, 37, 70
Article 13, 35, 38, 55, 70
Article 19, 3
Article 23, 56, 70
Article 24, 4
Article 27, 3
Article 28, 4, 35, 39, 70
Article 29, 19, 35, 55, 70, 85, 99–108
Article 31, 70, 90, 97
Article 42, 34
assessment 16, 17, 31, 33, 44–55, 58,
    63, 65, 66, 76, 100
assessment baseline, 50
assessment language of, 51
assumptions, 10
Audit Commission, 100

beliefs, 30
belonging, 29, 39
biased behaviour, 27
black educators, 32
books and book sharing, 87
British Association of Early
Childhood Education,
41

care of children, 27
challenge, 9, 23, 24, 31, 32, 92, 102
checklist, 30
child-centred, 38
child-rearing patterns and practices,
    31, 33
childhood, 8
childhood views of, 6
Children Act, 2, 13, 33, 97, 100
children's achievements, 44–55, 82, 83
children's attitudes, 18
children's autonomy, 34
children's best interests, 19, 20, 22, 50,
    64, 84, 106
children's capabilities, 34, 35, 39
children's civil rights, 6
children's competence, 15
children's control, 8
children's culture, 91
children's decision making, 7
children's development, 19, 25
children's environments, 40
children's ethnic identity, 25
children's feelings, 5, 24
children's growth, 40
children's home languages, 29, 30, 32,
    85, 86, 87, 102
children's human dignity, 35
children's individuality, 18, 26
children's interests, 41
children's knowledge, 18
children's learning and interactions,
    32, 34–43
children's linguistic development, 36
children's medical needs, 59
children's motivation, 16
children's needs, 11

children's opinions, 9, 35
children's perceptions of people, 27
children's personal frames of
  references, 36
children's personal identities, 25
children's personality, 35
children's powerlessness, 8
children's powers, 92
children's questions, 20
children's representations, 42
children's right to free education, 5
children's right to freedom from
  discrimination, 6
children's right to health, 5
children's right to life, 5
children's right to play, 5
children's right to privacy, 6
Children's Rights Development
  Unit, 2, 9
children's rights to survival and
  development, 6
children's skills, 18
children's socialisation, 28
children's spiritual, moral, social and
  cultural development, 20
children's status, 9
children's talents, 35
children's thinking, 42
children's underachievement, 27
children's understanding, 42
children's uniqueness, 67
children's views, 5, 9
children's welfare, 2
choice and choices, 9, 36
citizens and citizenship, 43, 55
civil rights, 1
class, class bias, class prejudice, 24,
  25, 26, 27
Code of Practice – special needs 2, 33,
  65, 66, 67
collaboration, 56, 66, 67, 68
communication, 39
community, 29, 32, 33, 39, 57, 60, 108
competence, 17
'confident mark', 101, 104
conformity, 102
consultation, 2
continuity, 42
contribution, 39
courtesy, 9
criminal responsibility, 4
cultural awareness, 32
cultural differences, 36

culture 31, 85, 104
curriculum, 14, 15, 16, 19, 21, 23, 31,
  33, 34–43, 45, 65, 82, 91, 92, 96,
  103, 107

decision making, 8, 33
democratic, 8
development, 14, 28, 57, 106, 107
developmental approach, 27
developmental curriculum, 40
developmental levels, 45
developmentally appropriate, 35
DFE, 78
difference, 26, 104
dignity, 103
disability, 26
discipline, 35
discrimination, 24
discussions, 36
disenfranchisement of children, 14
displays, 23
diversity, 31
documentation, 17

Early Childhood Education Forum, 99
Early Years Curriculum Group, 35
'education for life', 51
Education Reform Act, 35
educational needs, 57
educational theory, 34
educators' knowledge, 29
effective practice, 24
effectiveness, 100
efficiency, 11, 17
emotional development, 107
emotional learning, 42
emotional struggles, 47
emotions, 95
empowerment, 27, 39, 104, 105
English as a second language, 30
entitlement, 11, 14, 41
environments, 30
equality of opportunity, 23–33, 54
ethnic minority languages, 29
ethnicity, 26
ethos, 17, 32, 33, 36, 59, 92, 95
evidence, 16, 19, 20
exclusions, 4
expectations, 68
exploration, 39
expression, 97, 102

failing schools, 14

family, 8, 10, 33, 39, 49, 54, 62, 63, 67, 68, 84, 88, 96, 100
fear, 14, 15
festivals, 32, 85
flexibility, 15, 66
Freedom, 39
funding, 53

gender, 24, 25, 28
girls' performance 24
'good enough' 100

harassment, 33
health, 3
holistic, 103
holistic approach, 27
holistic development, 39
Home visiting, 86, 87
homelessness, 106
human rights, 1, 103
humiliation, 9

identity, 25, 26, 29, 108
Improvement, 11
inclusion, 24, 68
individual needs, 36
individuality, 35
ineffective practice, 24
inequality, 3, 24, 26
infant education, 12
Inspection, 11–22
inspection – 'light touch', 11, 69
integrated approach, 27
interaction, 18, 23, 29, 67, 102, 103
interactional contexts 24
interdisciplinary 64
international cooperation, 35, 39
intervention, 54, 56, 57, 66, 94, 105

Joint inspections, 13

knowledge, 34
knowledge of educators, 28

language, 40
language acquisition, 36
language awareness, 32
learner centred, 35
learning, 27, 36, 38
learning experiences, 34
learning opportunities, 46

legislation, 2
leisure, 90
levels – of Equal opportunities practice 30–33

management, 53
mathematical development, 40
media images, 27
Montessori education, 78
motivation, 43
multi cultural, 32
multi lingual, 32
multi-faith, 32
multi-professional, 38

National Children's Bureau, 99
National Commission on Education, 69
National Curriculum, 14, 27, 35, 52
National Vocational Qualifications, 73, 74, 75
neural connections, 42
nursery education, 11, 12, 38
Nursery nurses, 72, 73
nursery school, 36

Obligations, 6
observation, 17, 19, 31, 32, 41, 44–55, 94, 96, 102, 103
OFSTED, 11–22
OMEP, 87
opportunities, 91
opportunities for learning, 36
organisation, 40

paperwork, 16
parental views, 27
parenthood, 6
parents, 11, 17, 19, 30, 31, 32, 33, 44, 49, 57, 58, 65, 81–89, 100
participation, 41
partners, 59, 82
pedagogy, 38
personal and social education, 25
philosophy, 56, 61, 67, 68
planned learning, 38
planning, 34, 40
play, 8, 10, 18, 31, 34, 90–98, 100
playgroup, 36, 79, 91
policy/policies, 9, 17, 23, 27, 32, 89
positive action, 25
positive reinforcement, 43

poverty, 3, 84, 97
power – of educator, 50
power relations, 33
prejudice, 104
privacy, 9
problem solving, 41
procedures, 32
professional development, 16
professional knowledge, 14, 38
progress, 18, 35, 54
progressive, 14
promoting respect, 23
protection, 6, 16, 47, 54
punishment, 3, 9

quality, 11, 12, 15, 17, 34, 69, 89
quality of experiences, 54
Quality in Diversity, 38, 39
quality of education, 19
quality of learning, 15, 19
quality of relationships, 21
quality of teaching, 15, 19
questions and questioning, 36

race, 26
race esteem, 25
Race Relations Act, 33
racial identity, 25
racial ideology, 25
racism, 24, 25, 27, 28
reciprocal discussion, 41
record-keeping, 33, 41
recruitment, 33
Reggio Emilia, 39
relationships, 9, 16, 21, 36, 39, 43, 46,
    57, 66, 97, 103
religious education, 3
resources, 32, 33
responsibilities, 7, 8, 21, 34
responsibility, 7, 52, 62, 64
responsibility for learning, 38
responsibility of management, 33
role of the adult, 41

schemas, 42, 45, 46
Scottish Vocational Qualifications, 73,
    74
self-concept, 25
self-esteem, 24, 32
self-evaluation, 12, 16
self-image, 32
self-worth, 107

Sex Discrimination Act, 33
sex education, 3
sexism, 24, 27, 28
sexuality, 26
Sheffield Early Literacy Development
    project, 49
smacking, 6
social development, 107
social dimension of learning, 38
social learning, 28, 42
socialisation, 23
special educational needs, 17, 56–68
special learning needs, 32
special schools, 4
specialist teacher assistants, 77
spontaneous learning, 38
staff awareness, 32
staff development, 31, 32
staff training, 29
standards, 11, 17, 18, 19
standards of achievement, 14
statutory school age, 14
stereotypes, 27, 32, 45
subjects, 14
successful schools, 20

Te Whariki, 39
teacher training, 70, 71, 72
teachers, 15
teaching, 27
teaching methods, 14
technology, 53, 107
terminology, 51
time, 40, 53
timetables, 15
token measures, 31
tolerance, 24
traditional approach, 38
training, 46, 69–80

UN Convention, 1, 33
UN implementation, 3, 5
UN ratification, 1
underachievement, 24
understanding, 45

value for money, 19
value-added, 17, 18
valuing languages, 29
violence, 3, 48, 84
voucher, 11
vulnerability, 58, 107

Warnock Report, 33
well-being, 39
worthwhile, 50

zone of proximal development, 46